THE BISHOPS' SYNOD

ARCA

Classical and Medieval Texts Papers and Monographs 1

© 1976 M.J. Faris, R.H.M. Dolley. M.J. McGann, A.B. Scott, W.C. Kerr.

Published by Francis Cairns, School of Classics,
Abercromby Square. University of Liverpool, P.O. Box 147,
Liverpool L69 3BX   All rights reserved.

ISBN   0 905205 01   4

Printed in Great Britain in the Administrative Department of
The University of Liverpool.

THE BISHOPS' SYNOD

("THE FIRST SYNOD OF ST. PATRICK")

A Symposium
with Text Translation and Commentary

Edited by

M.J. FARIS

X

FRANCIS CAIRNS

Authors and Publisher

are indebted to the

INSTITUTE OF IRISH STUDIES

OF THE

QUEEN'S UNIVERSITY OF BELFAST

for a contribution towards

the cost of publication

of this volume

*

The editor thanks the Master and Fellows of Corpus Christi
College, Cambridge, for permission to reproduce photographs
of their Manuscript 279, pp. 1–11.

CONTENTS

INCIPIT SINODUS EPISCOPORUM
ID EST PATRICI AUXILII ISSERNINI

Gratias agimus Deo Patri et Filio et Spiritui Sancto.

Presbiteris et diaconibus et omni clero Patricius Auxilius Isserninus
5 episcopi salutem.

Satius nobis neglegentes praemonere culpare que facta sunt Solamone
dicente: melius est arguere quam irasci.

Exempla difinitionis nostrae inferius conscripta sunt et sic inchoant:

1. Si quis in questionem captivis quesierit in plebe suo iure sine permisi
10 meruit excommonicari.

2. Lectores denique cognoscant unus quisque aecclesiam in qua psallat.

3. Clericus vagus non sit in plebe.

4. Si quis permissionem acciperit et collectum sit praetium non plus
exigat quam quod necessitas poscit.

15 5. Si quid supra manserit ponat super altare pontificis ut detur ali
indigenti.

6. Quicumque clericus ab hostiario usque ad sacerdotem sine tunica
visus fuerit atque turpitudinem ventris et nuditatem non tegat, et si non
more Romano capilli eius tonsi sint, et uxor eius si non velato capite
20 ambulaverit, pariter a laicis contempnentur et ab ecclesia separentur.

7. Quicumque clericus ussus neglegentiae causa ad collectas mane vel
vespere non occurrerit alienus habeatur nisi forte iugo servitutis sit
detentus.

8. Clericus si pro gentili homine fideiusor fuerit in quacumque
25 quantitate et si contigerit, quod mirum non †potest, per astutiam aliquam
gentilis ille clerico fallat, rebus suis clericus ille solvat debitum. Nam si
armis conpugnaverit cum illo, merito extra ecclesiam conputetur.

9. Monachus et virgo unus abhinc et alia ab aliunde in uno hospitio non
conmaneant nec in uno curru a villa in villam discurreant nec adsidue
30 invicem confabulationem exerceant.

line 6   quam culpare (Spelman)
line 9   permisione (Ware)
line 25   non est (Ware)

1

THE BISHOPS' SYNOD

Introduction   Here begins the synod of the bishops, that is, of Patrick Auxilius Isserninus. We give thanks to God the Father and the Son and the Holy Spirit. To the priests and deacons and every cleric, the bishops Patrick, Auxilius, Isserninus, greetings.

To us it is more fit to warn the careless and to censure what has been done, as Solamon says, it is better to rebuke than to be wroth. Copies of our decision have been drawn up as under, and they begin thus:

Canon 1   If anyone on behalf of captives has quested in the community on his own authority without permission, he has deserved to be excommunicated.

Canon 2   Lastly let the lectors get to know, each one of them, the church in which he is to sing the psalms.

Canon 3   A wandering cleric shall not be in the community.

Canon 4   If any one has received permission and the price has been collected, he shall not exact more than need demands.

Canon 5   If anything is left over, he shall place it on the bishop's altar so that it may be given to another needy person.

Canon 6   Whatever cleric, from porter to bishop, has been seen without a tunic and does not cover the shame of his belly and his nakedness, and if his hair has been been cut after the Roman fashion, and if his wife has gone about unveiled, they shall equally be held in contempt by the laity, and let them be separated from the church.

Canon 7   Whatever cleric, when bidden, by reason of carelessness does not come to morning or evening prayers he shall be considered a stranger unless it happens that he has been held in the yoke of slavery.

Canon 8   If a cleric has stood surety for any amount for a pagan, and if it has happened, which cannot be surprising, that the pagan by some trick cheats the cleric, the cleric shall pay that which is due out of his own resources. For if he engages in armed combat with him he shall rightly be considered outside the church.

Canon 9   A monk and a virgin, he from here and she from elsewhere, shall not stay together in one guesthouse, nor shall they travel about in one carriage from settlement to settlement, nor shall they persist in carrying on conversation together.

10. Si incoeptum boni operis ostenderit in psallendo et nunc intermisit et comam habeat, ab ecclesia excludendus nisi statui priori se restituerit.

11. Quicumque clericus ab aliquo excommonicatus fuerit et alius eum susciperit, ambo coaequali penitentia utantur.

12. Quicumque Christianus excominicatus fuerit, nec eius elimosina recipiatur.

13. Elimosinam a gentibus offerendam in ecclesiam recipi non licet.

14. Christianus qui occiderit aut fornicationem fecerit aut more gentilium ad aruspicem iuraverit, per singula cremina annum penitentiae agat; impleto cum testibus veniat anno penitentiae et postea resolvetur a sacerdote.

15. Et qui furtum fecerit demedium peniteat, .xx. diebus cum pane, et si fieri potest rapta repraesentet; sic in ecclesiam renuetur.

16. Christianus qui crediderit esse lamiam in saeculo, quae interpraetatur striga, anathemazandus quicumque super animam famam istam inposuerit, nec ante in ecclesiam recipiendus quam ut idem creminis quod fecit sua iterum voce revocat et sic poenitentiam cum omni diligentia agat.

17. Virgo quae voverit Deo permanet kasta et postea nubserit carnalem sponsum excommonis sit donec convertatur; si conversa fuerit et dimiserit adulterium penitentiam agat et postea non in una domo nec in una villa habitent.

18. Si quis excommonis fuerit nec nocte pascharum in ecclesiam non introeat donec penitentiam recipiet.

19. Mulier Christiana quae acciperit virum honestis nuptis et postmodum discesserit a primo et iunxerit se adulterio, quae haec fecit excommonis sit.

20. Christianus qui fraudat debitum cuiuslibet ritu gentilium excommunis sit donec solvat debitum.

line 1	Si quis (Haddan and Stubbs)
line 9	aruspicem meaverit (Spelman)
line 14	in speculo (Spelman)
line 15	anathematizandus (Spelman)
line 17	revocet (Spelman). cat super cet (Prima manu?)
line 18	permanere (Wilkins)
line 20	adulterum (Wilkins). domo ex domu (Prima manu?)
line 25	adultero (Spelman)

Canon 10	If he has clearly begun the good work in singing psalms and has now broken off and has a full head of hair, he is to be shut out from the church unless he returns to the former state.
Canon 11	Whatever cleric has been excommunicated by someone, and another has received him back, both shall follow an equal penance.
Canon 12	Whatever Christian has been excommunicated, not even his alms shall be accepted.
Canon 13	It is not permissible for alms that may be offered by pagans to be received into the church.
Canon 14	A Christian who has killed or committed fornication or, in the manner of pagans, has sworn before a soothsayer shall spend a year of penance for each offence. When the year of penance has been completed he shall come with witnesses and then he will be set free by the bishop.
Canon 15	And the man who has committed theft shall do penance half a year, twenty days on bread, and if it can be done he shall return what he has stolen. Thus he will be re-admitted to the church.
Canon 16	A Christian who has believed that there is such a thing in the world as a lamia, that is to say a vampire, is to be put under the ban — whoever that is who has cast that slur upon a living soul — and he is not to be received back into the church before he retracts verbally the charge which he has made, and so does penance with all zeal.
Canon 17	A virgin who has vowed to God to (?) remain chaste and then has married a spouse in the flesh, she shall be excommunicate until she changes her way of life; if she has changed her way of life and has given up her adultery she shall do penance, and they shall not live thereafter in the one house nor in the one settlement.
Canon 18	If a man has been excommunicate, he shall not enter the church even on the night of Easter until he accepts penance.
Canon 19	A Christian woman who has taken a husband in valid marriage and afterwards has left the first man and has coupled herself adulterously, she who has done these things shall be excommunicate.
Canon 20	A Christian who defaults on what is, by pagan custom, anyone's due shall be excommunicate until he pays the due.

21. Christianus cui dereliquerit aliquis et provocat eum †imductum et non in ecclesiam ut ibi examinetur causa, qui sic fecerit alienus sit.

22. Si quis tradiderit filiam suam viro honestis nuptis et amaverit alium et consentit filiae suae et acceperit dotem, ambo ab aecclesia excludantur.

23. Si quis presbiterorum aecclesiam aedificaverit, non offerat antequam adducat suum pontificem ut eam consecret. quia sic decet.

24. Si quis advena ingressus fuerit plebem non ante baptizat neque offerat nec consecret nec aecclesiam aedificet nec permissionem accipiat ab episcopo, nam qui a gentibus sperat permissionem alienus sit.

25. Si que a religiosis hominibus donata fuerint diebus illis quibus pontifex in sigulis habitaverit aecclesis pontificalia dona, sicut mos antiquis ordinare, ad episcopum pertinebunt sive ad ussum necessarium sive aegentibus distribuendum, prout ipse episcopus moderabit.

26. Si quis vero clericus contravenerit et dona invadere fuerit depraehensus, ut turpis lucri cupidus ab ecclesia sequestretur.

27. Clericus aepiscopi in plebe quislibet novus ingresor, baptizare et offerre illum non licet nec aliquid agere; qui si sic non faciat excommonis sit.

28. Si quis clericorum excommonis, solus non in eadem domo cum fratribus orationem facit nec offere nec consecrare licet donec se faciat emendatum; qui si sic non fecerit, dupliciter vindicetur.

29. Si quis fratrum accipere gratiam Dei voluerit non ante baptizetur quam ut .xl.mum agat.

30. Aepiscopus quislibet qui de sua in alteram progreditur parruchiam nec ordinare praesumat nisi permissionem acceperit ab eo qui in suo principatum est. Die dominica offerat tantum susceptione et obsequi hic contentus sit.

line 1	in iudicium (Spelman). in duellum (Dolley)
line 8	quam permissionem (Spelman). donec permissionem acceperit (Ware)
line 11	singulis (Spelman)
line 13	moderabit ex noderabit (Prima manu?)
line 19	excommonis fuerit (Spelman). domo ex domu (Prima manu?)
line 20	faciat (Spelman). ei licet (Bieler)
line 25	acciperit ex acceperit (Prima manu?)

Canon 21	A Christian whom someone has wronged and who calls him forth . . . . and not to the church for the case to be considered there, he who does that shall be as a stranger.
Canon 22	If anyone has handed over his daughter to a man in valid marriage and she loves another and he is in agreement with his daughter and he accepts a bride price, both shall be shut out from the church.
Canon 23	If any priest has built a church, he shall not offer before bringing his own bishop to consecrate it, for so it is proper.
Canon 24	If any newcomer has come into a community he shall not baptize nor offer nor consecrate nor build a church until(?) he receives permission from the bishop, for he who expects permission from the people shall be a stranger.
Canon 25	If any gifts have been made by devout persons on those days on which the bishop resides in the several churches, these pontifical gifts, as was the custom for the ancients to prescribe, will belong to the bishop, whether for essential purposes or to be distributed to the needy, as the bishop himself will decide.
Canon 26	But if any cleric has disobeyed and has been caught making inroads on the gifts, he shall be cut off from the church as greedy for sordid gain.
Canon 27	Any cleric in a bishop's community who is a new arrival may not baptize or offer or perform any act. If he does not comply he should be excommunicate.
Canon 28	If any excommunicate cleric is praying alone and not in the same house with his brethren he may not either offer or consecrate until he has corrected himself. If he fails to comply with this, his punishment shall be doubled.
Canon 29	If one of the brothers wishes to receive the grace of God he shall not be baptized before he fulfils a forty-day fast.
Canon 30	Any bishop who goes from his own to another diocese shall neither (not, not even) presume to ordain unless he receives permission from him who is in his own jurisdiction; on Sunday he shall offer only by formal invitation and he shall be content to be subordinate while in this diocese.

31. Si quis conduxerit e duobus clericis quos discordare convenit per discordiam aliquam prolatum uni e duobus hostem ad interficiendum, homicida congruum est nominari; qui clericus ab omnibus rectis habetur alienus.

5 32. Si quis clericorum voluerit iuvare captivo, cum suo praetio illi subveniat. Nam si per furtum illum inviolaverit, blasfemantur multi clerici per unum latronem. Qui sic fecerit excommonis sit.

33. Clericus qui de Britanis ad nos venit sine epistola, etsi habitet in plebe, non licitum ministrare.

10 34. Diaconus nobiscum similiter qui inconsultu suo abbate sine litteris in aliam parruchiam †adsentiat, nec cibum ministrare decet et a suo presbitero quem contempsit per penitentiam vindicetur.

Et monachus inconsultu abbate vagulus decet vindicari.

FINIUNT SINODI DISTITUTA

line 6   involaverit (Salmasius apud Wilkins)
line 11   absentat (Ware)
line 14   STATUTA (Bieler)

Canon 31   If any one of two clerics who, it is agreed, are at odds has hired an enemy to one of the two induced by some quarrel to kill, it is appropriate that he should be named murderer. This cleric is considered a stranger by all righteous people.

Canon 32   If any cleric wishes to help a captive he shall come to his aid with his own honour price. For if he by stealth .... him, many clerics are reviled because of one robber. He who does this shall be excommunicate.

Canon 33   A cleric who comes to us from the Britains without a letter, although he may be resident among the people, is not permitted to serve.

Canon 34   A deacon with us likewise who not consulting his own abbot .... without a letter into another parish, should not serve food, and he shall be punished with penance by his own priest whom he has slighted.

And a monk wandering without consulting the abbot should be punished.

The decisions of the synod end.

INTRODUCTION

It might seem unnecessary, not to say impertinent, to produce an edition of *The Bishops' Synod* so soon after the publication of Professor Bieler's edition[1] and in spite of extensive comment on the *Synod* by him, Professor Binchy and Dr. Kathleen Hughes.[2] Indeed, when a working party of the Ulster Society for Medieval Latin Studies began some time ago to make an intensive study of the *Synod*, it had no intention at all of publishing anything. Rather, its aim might have been described as an exercise in self-education through the examination of a document which clearly was a very rich mine of material for the student of early Christian Ireland, whether his interest lay in Hiberno-Latin, in civil and ecclesiastical organization and law, or in the social customs of the period, whatever the period was.

We therefore obtained a photo-copy of the manuscript, and relying heavily on Professor Bieler's edition, we made our own text and translation, compiling notes and queries on the way: at one stage we had the privilege of a joint visit by Professor Bieler and Professor Binchy to answer some of our questions in person.

When we proceeded to review what we had done, we realised that our text and translation differed in a number of respects from those of Professor Bieler and other scholars. Perhaps the main difference was that where the manuscript seemed to us to make no sense at all we did not feel obliged to force sense out of it against the run of the evidence. But there were many instances where we felt that previous translations assumed too readily that there was no doubt about both the general and the particular sense of the Latin. Rightly or wrongly, we came to the conclusion that many of the words and expressions of individual canons and whole canons themselves were not meaningful because the exact connotation of Latin words in successive periods of the history of early Christian Ireland had not been established: our view is that much further research in a number of related fields is needed before the thirty-four canons of the *Synod* can be understood and placed in a social and historical context. It seems to us much too early to come to any conclusion about the unity of the *Synod*, until its components make better sense.

We presented our text, translation and some papers on the *Synod* to an invited audience at a meeting in Queen's University, which literally was a symposium, and we now venture to publish the same material together with a full commentary to a wider audience. We have called our work '*The*

Bishops' Synod' because it is so entitled in the manuscript. Our debt to Bieler, Binchy and Hughes will be obvious to the reader, but we take this opportunity of acknowledging it with gratitude. We make no claim at all to have advanced the frontiers of knowledge, but we think that it may be of some value to make a record of the doubts and difficulties which have occurred to us in our effort to interpret the *Synod.*

W.C. Kerr

NOTES

1. *The Irish Penitentials*, 1963.

2. E.g. Bieler in *Mélanges offertes à C. Mohrmann*, 1963, and in *A History of Irish Catholicism* I, 1, 1967; Binchy in *Studia Hibernica* 2 (1962) and 8 (1968); Hughes, *The Church in Early Irish Society*, 1966.

MANUSCRIPT: CORPUS CHRISTI COLLEGE, CAMBRIDGE, NUMBER 279

The text of *The Bishops' Synod* is found in only one medieval manuscript. This is Manuscript 0.20 in the library of Corpus Christi College, Cambridge, which has the number 279 in the catalogue of Corpus manuscripts compiled by M.R. James.[1] The sixth canon is found in another Corpus manuscript, No 265, of the eleventh century, which like 279 came from Worcester Cathedral. It must, surely, have been copied from that manuscript.

Scholars from the sixteenth century onwards have used Manuscript 279, but it was the great liturgist, Henry Bradshaw, who first described the contents of the whole manuscript. He was also the first to notice that there were a number of manuscripts in various libraries each containing the same penitential manuals, and that these penitentials were all the product of one or other part of the Celtic Church. The result of his investigations into these manuscripts is incorporated in a long letter, dated May 1885, written to F.W. Wasserschleben who had produced − over thirty years previously − his monumental work on the penitentials of the Medieval Church,[2] and was now engaged in revising his edition of the collection of canon law, the so-called *Collectio Hibernensis*.[3] This letter is printed by Wasserschleben in his preface to that edition, and also separately as one of the two papers which go to make up Bradshaw's little book entitled *The Early Collection of Canons Known as the Hibernensis* (Cambridge, 1893). In it, Bradshaw pointed out that five of the manuscripts containing the *Collectio Hibernensis* were certainly written in Brittany. All five have Breton glosses. In three, the scribe is named, and the name is a Breton one. All of these manuscripts have a text of the *Collectio Hibernensis*. They also all contain the *Canones Wallici* and the *Canones Adomnani*. On the fringe of this group there are several other manuscripts loosely connected to it, and our manuscript is one of these. It contains extracts from the 'A' version of the *Collectio Hibernensis*, and also extracts from the Old Testament law, usually referred to as the *Liber de Lege Moysi*, which is found in three of the manuscripts just mentioned. But it does not have a fuller text of the *Collectio Hibernensis*, the *Canones Wallici* or the *Canones Adomnani*. This manuscript is undoubtedly related to the group of Breton manuscripts. Whether one can go further and say with Bradshaw 'the present manuscript . . . . owes its origin to manuscripts then preserved in Brittany' is more doubtful. There are no features in the manuscript itself

11

that would suggest that it had been copied from a Breton manuscript. The one point which might favour this is that the *Liber de Lege Moysi* found in this manuscript appears only in the five Breton manuscripts grouped together by Bradshaw.

This brings us on to discuss the date of the manuscript and the locality in which it was written. Bradshaw began his description with the words 'this is another manuscript of which it is very difficult to give in a few words a thoroughly satisfactory account'. I have had the opportunity of seeing it once only, and have otherwise had to use the photostat kindly provided by the librarian of Corpus Christi College.

Bradshaw and, following him, M.R. James dated the manuscript to the end of the ninth or beginning of the tenth century. Without any real evidence he supposed that it might have been written in the Low Countries. More recently, Professor Bischoff has given his opinion that it was written on the Continent near Tours or in some monastery under the influence of Tours. He too dates it to the second half of the ninth century.[4] There are some Irish glosses later on in this manuscript, and the way in which these have been garbled by the scribe indicates that it was written in Britain or on the Continent rather than in Ireland or in any Continental monastery where there was still a strong Irish tradition. On the other hand, the initial 'GRA' is not Continental or Turonian in appearance but insular, and indeed is not unlike some of the initials in the *Book of Durrow*. But, of course, the illuminator may have been copying from an insular original. The half uncial on that same first page is certainly much more like what one would expect to see in a Turonian manuscript. So it looks as if the manuscript is of Continental provenance, though written somewhere which had strong links with the Celtic world. We know nothing about the whereabouts of this manuscript in the early Middle Ages, but another Corpus manuscript, a copy of this text made from this manuscript for Archbishop Parker, is headed *Ex libro quodam vetusto ecclesiae Wigornensis*. This makes it clear that Parker 'borrowed' this manuscript from the library at Worcester Cathedral and that at his death in 1575 it went, with the rest of his books, to his own college where it still is (James No 298).

Our manuscript is of modest size (10½" x 7") and is probably all written in one hand. At least, so thought Bradshaw and James, although on looking at the actual manuscript, I thought I detected a change of hand at page 24, with the first hand coming back at page 84. But in any case the first part of the manuscript containing the *Synod* is in one hand. Even if there is a change of hand later on, the book is complete and all of one piece without later additions. As one would expect of a manuscript of this date, the ruling is dry point rather than crayon. There are curious triangles of dots in the right-hand margins. These are in addition to the normal prickings made in ruling the guide-lines which are, as one would expect, in dry-point. The 'triangles', on the other hand, are in the same ink as the text. There is some underlining on page 3. The first four of these were made by Parker or his scribe in the brown-red crayon which is the distinguishing mark of so many Parker manuscripts. This same crayon has also supplied the large pagination. But the last three underlinings at the foot of the page are in the ink used in the text. Apart from the first two pages this is a very plain manuscript. It has plain, unadorned initials, mostly red, but a few in black. The title page has capitals of which alternate lines are red and black. There is the same alteration on the verso of that leaf for the first five lines down to *salutem*. The red has oxydized very badly on the initials of the first leaves. It has also eaten into the parchment. The first three letters of *Gratias* are filled in with green.

The text of *The Bishops' Synod* occupies only the first five leaves. There are three other works in the manuscript. First of all (p 6), there is a collection of *sententiae* or *auctoritates* on church law and morals of a kind common at all periods of the Middle Ages. The principal sources cited by name are Gregory the Great, Isidore, Jerome, Cassiodorus, Origen, Gregory Nazianzen, with many biblical and especially Pauline quotations. Bieler and Bradshaw both regard this as containing the same kind of material as lies behind the *Collectio Hibernensis* (see Bieler, *Penitentials,* p 23). Then there is the *Liber de Lege Moysi*, followed on page 155 by sections IV and V of the *Canones Hibernenses* (Bieler, *Penitentials* pp 170-174) which, in turn, are followed by extracts from the 'A' version of the *Collectio Hibernensis*.

A.B. Scott

NOTES

1.   *A Descriptive Catalogue of the Manuscripts in the Library of Corpus Christi College*, 1912, II, p 42.

2.   *Bussordnung der abendländischen Kirche nebst einer rechtsgeschichtlichen Einleitung,* 1851.

3.   *Die irische Kanonensammlung*, 2nd ed. Leipzig, 1885.

4.   As quoted by Bieler, *Penitentials*, p 15.

THE HISTORY OF THE TEXT

The first scholar to use our text, or something like it, appears to have been the collector or compiler of the *Collectio Hibernensis*, who attributes to Patrick thirteen of the canons recorded in our manuscript, along with the quotation of the non-Vulgate version of *Ecclesiasticus* 20, 1, which heads it. He also cites No 20 of our manuscript which he attributes to a *Sinodus Romana*, and No 31, which he attributes to a *Sinodus Kartaginensis*. Unfortunately, in no case is the citation in the *Hibernensis* identical with the text of our manuscript. It is clear from the introduction to the *Hibernensis* (Wasserschleben, p 1) that the anthologist felt free to prune, expand, or improve his material, and it may well have been owing to his editing of his source, that his version usually presents a more polished, or indeed more readily intelligible text. From this, it has followed that while we have used the *Hibernensis* to help us elucidate the sense of our manuscript, we have not been able to offer a clear account of the relationship of the two texts. Indeed, this may not be possible until a fuller account than Wasserschleben's is available of the family of manuscripts which he classes as his 'B' text.

The next appearance known to us of our text is also in manuscript — Manuscript No 298 at Corpus Christi College, Cambridge, and is a transcript, made, one assumes, by a member of Archbishop Parker's secretariat of the first page-and-a-half of our manuscript down to Canon 6, which, with its reference to a priest's wife, would naturally be of interest to a sixteenth-century controversialist. After that, the scribe seems to have wearied in his task, and decided to transcribe only those canons that took his fancy — namely Nos 9 and 17. He concludes his extract with the first half of the last canon, perhaps to indicate the end of the document. More interesting, however, is his note at the head of the extract, *Ex libro quodam vetusto ecclesiae Wigornensis*, which throws some light on the provenance of the manuscript. Henry Bradshaw imagined it to have been written in the Low Countries or in Brittany, and to have come to Worcester in the baggage of some Norman bishop. The name Worcester has suggested Bishop Patrick as a possible connecting link.

We come now to the printed editions. These fall into two categories, collections of conciliar documents relating either to the Churches of the British Isles, or to the Western Church at large, and collections of Latin writings attributed to St Patrick. Our manuscript first appears in print in the collection of decrees, laws, etc, relating to the British Church, published by H. Spelman, London 1639. This is a good example of seventeenth-century editing, with much of the spelling of the manuscript altered to conform with contemporary fashion, or perhaps only with the fancy of the transcriber. On the other hand, many of his conjectures have been accepted by most later editors. To Spelman we owe, for example, the insertion of *quam* in the preamble, the change from *adulterio* to *adultero* in Canon 19, and the reading *in iudicium* for *imductum* in Canon 21. Suggestions of his that have not found general acceptance are: the punctuation in Canon 8 *fallat rebus suis*, instead of *rebus suis . . . solvat debitum*; and in Canon 7 *usus negligentiae causa*, 'using the excuse of negligence'. Suggestions of his that have found favour only with some editors, are: in Canon 16 *in speculo* for *in saeculo* as the dwelling-place of the *lamia*; and in Canon 14 *meaverit* 'has gone to' for *iuraverit* 'has sworn before'. To Spelman also, we owe the title *First Synod of St Patrick*, although the title-page of our manuscript in extra large letters calls it *The Bishops' Synod*. He dates it to 450-456, and says it must be later than St. Germain's *Synod of St Albans*, which he dates to 429. He argues also that, if Patrick and Palladius went to Ireland in 429 or 430 or 432 (these were the dates favoured by the historians of his day and earlier), this Synod could not have taken place until many years after the arrival of these first missionaries.

The next edition with significant alteration, that of D. Wilkins, London 1737, is little improvement on Spelman, but it has some points of interest. In Canon 7 he omits the difficult word *ussus* and records in his *apparatus* Salmasius's conjecture *iniusta*. He explains his deletion of the word as the brilliant conjecture of his friend, John Walker, Archdeacon of Hereford, who for this and other emendations, has received Wilkins' thanks, and will receive the far greater gratitude of the Republic of Letters. The notion is that *ussus* is dittography from the last syllable of *clericus*. More tantalising, however, is his mention of Salmasius (Claude de Saumaise) and his mention of other emendations to Canons 8, 15, 18 and 32, that he attributes to him. Salmasius will probably best be known as the target of two of Milton's shorter Latin poems, among the latest examples of British, if we may not call it Medieval, Latin. But Salmasius's works take up 10 columns of the British Museum Catalogue of printed books, and none of those there recorded appears to have anything to do with the *First Synod of St. Patrick*, so we have to confess that we have not been able to discover where Salmasius recorded his emendations.

So far as we have been able to gather, most of the larger collections of Church Councils have been content to reproduce Spelman, sometimes with the conjectures of Wilkins and Ware, and so they need not detain us. Haddan and Stubbs, Oxford 1878, may perhaps merit a brief examination, since they raise the question of dating, and it seems from their notes that they had collated the manuscript. Previous editors, including Ware and Villanueva, appear to have accepted the attribution to Patricius, Auxilius and Isserninus. Haddan and Stubbs, following their own interpretation of Canons 6 and 33, think that the document must relate to a period when the British and Irish Churches were estranged, when the Irish had accepted Roman customs but the British still held to Celtic customs, ie, at least after 716 but before 777 or 809 — the early years of the eighth century being the earliest date that can be assigned to the document as a whole. While the working party had strong reservations about accepting the attribution to Patrick and the other two bishops, we did not think that the two canons mentioned need bear the interpretation put on them by Haddan and Stubbs.

We turn now to the other tradition of printed editions — that of collections of the works attributed to St Patrick. The *editio princeps* in this respect is Ware, London 1656 — a very rare book of which we finally found a copy in the library of the Presbyterian College, Belfast, and we are most grateful to the Principal and Professors for the opportunity of collating it. In fact, Ware does not contribute much. In his introduction he speaks respectfully of Spelman's edition, and his own few variants and glosses are not of great interest.

Of more interest is the first annotated edition, that of J.L. Villanueva, Dublin 1835. Of his 400-page edition of the works attributed to St Patrick, the first 100 are devoted to our document. His text is not remarkable. It is Spelman with Ware and Wilkins, and Villanueva does not seem to have examined the manuscript himself. His notes in Latin are very discursive, rather like a set of lecture notes by a university teacher who wanders from the exegesis of the matter in hand, to discuss points which he imagines will interest or educate his students. Writing when Celtic studies had not yet attained their present respectable position, and indeed, before Gaelic was classed as an Indo-European language, he likes to derive Irish names from Hebrew, and to illustrate primitive Irish customs from a supposed Phoenician origin. On the other hand, he records that the Patrician date for Canon 6, which appears to recommend the Roman tonsure, had already been questioned by John Lanigan, who had held that the canon in question cannot be earlier than 633 (when the South of Ireland accepted the Roman Easter), and indeed, Lanigan thought that this canon might be as late as the eighth century. Villanueva, who is convinced that the document is wholly Patrician, has at this point a long discussion in which he satisfied himself that in Patrick's time any distinction in the shape of tonsure would have been between a Western or Roman form, (whether circular, or *ab aure ad aurem*), and the Greek tonsure favoured by the Eastern Church, probably a total shaving of the head. One could wish that Bury had considered Villanueva's evidence before going off in pursuit of Druids.

Again, in 'St Patrick and the Coming of Christianity', (pp 88f.), Professor Bieler puts forward a new interpretation of Canon 29, stating that it prescribes a minimum age of 40 for baptism. We, though somewhat perplexed by the gender of *quadragesimum* (Spelman had expanded it to *quadragintesimum*) had agreed with Professor Bieler's earlier interpretation in his edition of the *Penitentials* 'let him not be baptised before he keeps a 40-day fast'. But more than 100 years ago, Villanueva had already considered and rejected that view that *quadragintesimum agat* meant 39 years of age.

We are, of course, very much indebted to Professor Bieler, not only for his many contributions to the literature of our document, but also especially for his edition, published in his collection of *Irish Penitentials*. Our only criticism of his text is that it conceals the difficulty and, indeed, perversity, of some of the Latin and so makes the document appear a surer authority on which to base conjectures about the nature of the early Irish Church than in fact it is. For this reason, in preparing our text for publication, we have chosen to relegate conjectures from Spelman onwards to the *apparatus* and to reproduce as nearly as possible what was written by the scribe. Spelman, in his introduction, described our manuscript as *malesanum implorans criticorum sagacitatem*, and Wilkins had called the writing *aegri vix sanabiles sine critica licentia*. Now the handwriting is anything but *malesanum*. Indeed, it is rather beautiful and quite easy to read, but the sense of these canons is certainly obscure and invites critical licence.

The literature, like the editions, again is divided between church history and Patrician studies. We were not able to agree on a firm date for this document, but were, on the whole, inclined to think it was not, Patrician. For those who do think it Patrician and who think Patrick learned his churchmanship in Gaul, one of the books on church history raises a difficulty that has not often been considered. Gaudemet in *L'Eglise dans l'Empire Romain* assumes that our *Synod* is Patrician, but, when he cites it, it is usually for some feature not readily paralleled in the Church of Gaul, with which he is mainly concerned. This would seem to

17

suggest either that our document is not Patrician, or that Patrick did not bring a Gallic church to Ireland, As we, on the whole, incline to the former view, we can leave aside the Patrician question and consider what our document has to say to Irish historians. Here a further problem arises. Is this, as it purports to be, a genuine piece of ecclesiastical legislation, whatever its date may be, or is it a collection of canons, perhaps of differing dates and provenance, made either for antiquarian interest or for polemical purposes, perhaps to commend the episcopal rather than the abbatical form of church government? Professor Binchy, in his article in *Studia Hibernica* 2 (1962), argues strongly for the essential unity of the document, although he utterly rejects its attribution to Patrick, and although he agrees that it is probably the production of the Reform, or Romanising, Party of the sixth or mid-seventh century. This essay also provides a succinct account of the literature of this document in connexion with the Patrician Question. We have, on the whole, tended to the view that this is not a genuine single piece of legislation, but more like a collection. Dr. K. Hughes, however, in her masterly *The Church in Early Irish Society*, seems to hold a middle ground, and may well be right. She argues for a sixth-century date, but holds that our document is based on an early group of canons which, because they were known to be ancient, were attributed to Patrick, and were re-issued in the seventh century, together with some alterations and additions, when the case for a diocesan clergy as against a monastic church must have been debated.

M.J. Faris

SOME LINGUISTIC PROBLEMS

The Latin word *plebs* accusative/ablative *plebe(m)*, with dropping of the final syllable, gave first /pleiβ/ in British Latin (the last consonant being a bilabial fricative) and Romano-British, which passed – presumably through the intermediate stage /plᴓiv/ – to become /pluɨv/, this being the present Welsh pronunciation, orthographically *plwyf*. In Breton, at all events in pretonic position in place-names, it was shortened to /plu/, orthographically *plou*. The Welsh word *plwyf* means 'parish' as we now understand this. In Italian the word *plebs* has become *pieve* 'parish church', but it does not seem to have survived in the other Romance languages. In the sixteenth century all the latter adopted the Latin word in the literary form *plebe* to denote 'populace' in the classical Latin sense.

Romano-British /pleiβ/, so far as I can trace, was not adopted into Irish. If it had come in very early it would have become **cliabh*, with substitution of Gaelic /q/, later *c* for British *p* as in loanwords of the so-called *Cothriche* group (the latter word being an early gaelicization of *Patricius* as opposed to the later Irish *Pádraig* which came in from early Welsh after Irish had acquired *p* by its own internal phonological development). There is, in fact, a word *cliabh* but it means 'basket' and has apparently no connection with *plebs*. Its diminutive *cléibhín* has passed into Ulster English as *claivin* 'bird-trap'. If the word had come into Irish later, after the latter had acquired *p* and when Welsh /ei/ had become /uɨ/ then its form would be Old Irish **pluib* or **ploeb*, or modern **plaobh*, which does not exist.

Latin *paruchia* or *paroechia* (whence French *paroisse* and English *parish*) is the source of Irish *pairche*, later also *fairche*, which means 'diocese'. Irish *paroíste* (parish) and *deoghais* or *deois* (diocese) are later borrowings of the Anglo-Norman period.

Latin *populus* has given Irish *pobal*, 'a people, tribe or congregation, a parish' (Dinneen). This is one of the later-type loans (of the *Pádraig* group) through Welsh *pobl*. In Spanish *pueblo* and Portuguese *pobo* 'village', we see what is basically the same semantic development. French *peuple* is a semi-learned form, likewise Italian *popolo* (post-Carolingian, not a direct colloquial development of *populus*). In Irish *teach pobail* is a Catholic chapel. *Pobal* also occurs in the barony name *Pobal Bhriain* (Pubblebrien) in County Limerick.

It would appear from this that before *paruchia* changed its meaning from 'diocese' to 'parish', there were two Latin words used in the latter sense: *populus* in the western periphery (Irish, *pobal*; Spanish, *pueblo*; Portuguese, *pobo*) and *plebs* in a more central area (whence Italian, *pieve*; Welsh, *plwyf*). From this, two rival arguments could be put forward:

1. Since *populus/pobal* was the peripheral term for 'parish', the Latin *plebs* was free to be used in a wider sense or, at least, a different sense, eg, perhaps = *tuath*.

2. *Plebs* was not, in fact, used in this wider sense and its use in the document under discussion, probably in the sense of 'parish' is, therefore, an argument for late composition by some purveyor of British Latin in which *plebs* had ousted *populus* of the peripheral area, which one could expect in Hiberno-Latin of an earlier period.

These chronological arguments are based on the principle, generally valid in linguistic geography, that older forms and meanings tend to survive in peripheral areas. Professor Dolley wants *plebs* to represent *tuath*, which, if true, might fit the first argument, but he also thinks the document is late, which would fit the second. Apart from this inconsistency, it seems to me that *tuath* stands for something that is too large for the size of population group that *plebs* evidently represented if in late Latin it had acquired the meaning it has in the only languages that have carried it on as a colloquial word — Italian with its *pieve* 'parish church' and Welsh with its *plwyf* 'parish'. Dinneen defines *tuath* as a population group capable of maintaining 3,000 (or less, down to 700 according to McNeill) soldiers in emergency. Assuming men capable of bearing arms to be about one-fourth of the total population in those times, that would mean that the *tuath* had a population of from 2,800 to 12,000. The baronies of Norman and modern times represent the ancient *tuatha*, more or less. Around 1660, according to Petty's census, barony populations varied from just over 5,000 down to about 400, but this was immediately after a period of war and after several centuries of subdivision. It seems unlikely that *plebs* as an ecclesiastical term would have applied to an area as large as this implies, and that it must be construed in the narrower ecclesiastical sense of 'parish' as we now understand this.

Tuath in later times acquired the secondary meanings 'people or folk, the laity' and in the first element of compounds it carried the meanings 'left-hand, rustic, clumsy, magic'. Its semantic development is not unlike that of Latin *paganus*, and it might be suggested that *gentes* rather than *plebs* was likely to be its Latin equivalent. The loaded meaning of *gentibus* as 'pagans' in Canon 13 does not invalidate that equivalence; in fact, it rather strengthens it. One would have to see how *tuath* is translated in early Irish texts where both languages are used, eg, *Annals of Ulster*, or how such words as *gentes, plebs, populus* are glossed in Old Irish. *Tuath* is represented in the Germanic languages by Old English *theode* (surviving in the place-name *Thetford* 'people's ford'), by German *deut(sch)*, and in the first syllable of the Latin adjective *Teutonicus*, so it is of Indo-European origin, common to Celtic and Germanic languages. Several *tuatha* could be grouped together to form a *mór-thuath* and several of the latter formed each of the five *cóicid* or fifths, which are the basis of the four modern provinces. When the present system of dioceses was fixed in the twelfth century they generally corresponded to the *mór-thuatha* rather than the *tuatha*.

I have looked through the Latin texts given in Strachan's *Old Irish Glosses* and Thurneysen's *Old Irish Reader*, without however, finding any instance of either *plebs* or *populus*. In Strachan, Old Irish *popul* (modern *pobal*) occurs in several glosses but unfortunately these are all instances where he does not give the Latin of the text glossed. The sense in which the word is used seems to be sometimes 'people' in general and sometimes 'congregation' (ie, parish in a demographic rather than a geographic sense). I have also looked through the first volume of the *Annals of Ulster* without finding anything helpful except one instance under the year 1020 reading in Irish '*Amalgaid i comarbus Patraic doreir tuathi agus eclaisi*' translated '*Amhalgaidh* in the successorship of Patrick by the will of the laity and clergy'. This shows *tuath* used in the sense of 'laity' and in this sense it might, perhaps, be the equivalent of *plebs*. The point which I think we need to make is that while *tuath* and *plebs* might be equivalents when used in a demographic sense, meaning 'laity' as opposed to 'clergy', this equivalence ceases when they are used in a geographic sense, because then *tuath* means 'kingdom' whereas *plebs* probably means 'parish' and it is highly unlikely that the two were in any way comparable areas.

In Old Irish the term *geinti* occurs for Gentiles and was sometimes applied to the pagan Norsemen.

If the word *populus* had come into Irish as one of the *Cothriche* type loanwords its form would have been *cochal. There is, in fact, such a word, but with double 'l', namely *cochall* 'hood', which has passed into Ulster English as *coghal*, the name for the type of net used by the Bann fishermen, but this is a loan from Latin *cucullus*.

Perhaps now I can try to sum all this up in sequence.

1.   The Latin terms for 'diocese' and 'parish' in the late-fourth or early-fifth century seem to have been respectively *paruchia* and either *plebs* or *populus* according to region, both the latter retaining also their more general sense of 'people'. Of these, the first became established in Irish as *pairche* or *fairche*.

2.   If either *plebs* or *populus* had become established as loanwords in Irish during the *Cothriche* period of word-borrowing they would have become **cliabh* and **cochal* respectively, the first of which would have formed a homonym with the native word for 'basket' and the second a near homonym with another loanword meaning 'hood'. Is the absence of such loanwords due to the desirability of avoiding such semantic collisions or to the absence in early Christian Ireland of the institution in question, which might have been the case if, in fact, the *pairche* was as small a unit as the modern parish?

3.   If either *plebs* or *populus* became established as loanwords in Irish during the *Pádraig* period of word-borrowing, they would have become respectively **plaobh* (which did not happen) and *pobal* (which did happen).

4.   Of the Romance and Celtic languages that have preserved one or other of these words in spoken use, Italian has preserved *plebs* in its ecclesiastical meaning; Spanish and Portuguese have preserved *populus* generally with a secular meaning; Welsh has preserved both the same division of meanings (respectively as *plwyf*/parish and *pobl*/people) and Irish has taken over Welsh *pobl* as *pobal* with both meanings.

5.   In so far as *plebs* was used by later Latin writers – at least in the Celtic countries, and perhaps even in the Romance countries – in an ecclesiastical context, one would expect it to be used in the sense which it developed in the local colloquial speech, namely, 'parish'.

6.   If the word is to be understood in this sense, then its occurrence suggests a Welsh rather than an Irish origin for the writer of the document under discussion, and a sufficiently late date for the colloquial derivatives of *plebs* and *populus* to have become differentiated in meaning.

7.   If, on the other hand, *plebs* is to be understood in its original and less specific sense, then it must mean 'laity' as opposed to 'clergy', and if its Irish equivalent is *tuath* the latter can only be understood likewise in this secondary sense and not in its original sense of people as a political kingdom.

G.B. Adams

A RECONSIDERATION OF SOME LINGUISTIC EVIDENCE

Professor Binchy's case against the authenticity of *The Bishops' Synod* rests, in part, on linguistic arguments.[1] The two studies by Professor Bieler which were written in response to Binchy's article have dealt with these arguments and added to their number.[2] The present paper has been written in the belief that further consideration of the linguistic evidence cited by both scholars is called for.

I Patrick's Latin and the Latin of the Canons

Binchy argues that the contrast between the 'arid but generally correct Latin' of the canons and the 'passionate, stumbling sentences of Patrick himself' in the *Confessio* and the *Epistle to Coroticus* is so great that it is impossible to believe that the first comes from the same hand as the other two.[3] Bieler had anticipated this point by suggesting that Patrick, working as a 'canonist', had followed certain 'models which greatly influenced his style' or that the decrees, though issued with his sanction, were not necessarily composed by him.[4] Though Binchy dismissed these explanations,[5] they are, in fact, entirely reasonable, and Bieler is fully justified in continuing to regard them as valid.[6]

In any case Binchy's description of the language of the *Epistle* and the *Confessio* stands in need of qualification, and Bieler was right to recall Professor Christine Mohrmann's distinction between the relative fluency with which Patrick discusses 'religious subjects' and in particular 'the apostolic or missionary field' and the clumsiness of his narration of 'every day facts'.[7] The *Epistle* contains one passage where Patrick is, as it were, legislating, though with greater passion than would be manifested in the drawing up of a legal code: *quopropter resciat omnis homo timens Deum quod a me aliena sunt et a Christo Deo meo . . . . unde ergo quaeso plurimum, sancti et humiles corde, adulari talibus non licet nec cibum nec potum sumere cum ipsis nec elemosinas ipsorum recipi debeat donec crudeliter per paenitentiam effusis lacrimis satis Deo faciant et liberent servos Dei et ancillas Christi baptizatas, pro quibus mortuus est et crucifixus (epi 5 and 7).* The echoes here of Canons 7,21,24 and 31 (*'alienus sit (habeatur)* is rare in the *Irish Penitentials'*[8]) of Canons 12 and 13 and of Canons 18 and 28[9] are interesting though not highly significant. What is of importance is that this passage confirms what ought never to have been doubted — that Patrick, a bishop of the Western Church, was capable of laying down rules in 'generally correct Latin' for the government of his church. The nature of the language of the document

23

does not preclude its having been drawn up by the author of the *Epistle* and the *Confessio.*

II Hibernicisms in the Canons?

Binchy and Bieler are in agreement that the canons contain Hibernicisms. For Binchy, who believes that the document must stand or fall as a whole,[10] their presence proves that the whole document is late; for Bieler, that the canons in which they occur are late.[11]

Binchy claims that to understand the expression *Christianus qui . . . ad aruspicem iuraverit* in Canon 14, it is necessary to recall the use in Irish of the preposition *do* with the verb *tongid* 'swear'.[12] His statement is accepted by Bieler.[13] The present writer, a Latinist with a very limited knowledge of Irish, would like to see a connection established in detail. The article *tongaid* in the Royal Irish Academy's *Contributions to a Dictionary of the Irish Language*[14] shows that the preposition is used in formulas of asseveration, eg, *tonga do dia toinges mo thuath* 'I swear to God to whom my *tuath* swears'[15] and in situations where A swears to B in the sense that he gives him an undertaking under oath, eg, *Tuingsead uile dá éis sin . . . don rígh-se d'aitheasg éin-fhir/diamdaois coimh-neart síol na bhfear . . . nabdaois coimh-cheart ré chloinn-sean.* 'They all then swore to the king . . . that . . . they never would have equal claims with his race.' (*Contentio* xv, 45, translation by L. McKenna). It does not seem that *ad aruspicem iurare* conforms to either of these types, for the *aruspex* is apparently an institutionalised witness who validates the oath sworn in his presence.[16] There is, in any case, no need to have recourse to Irish usage: *ad aliquem* is commonly used in Latin with verbs denoting the making of formal statements to signify 'in somebody's presence';[17] *iurare ad* is found in Cato's *De Agricultura* (second century BC), where he says that olive pickers must swear before the owner of the farm (*iuranto ad dominum*) that they have not stolen any (144).[18] For the use of *iurare ad* in a context not very different from that of Canon 14, it is possible to cite Canon 16 of the Fourth Council of Orleans (AD 541), which lays down penalties for any Christian who follows pagan custom by swearing *ad caput cuiuscumque ferae vel pecudis* 'beside the head of any beast or farm animal'.

Canons 5 and 11 may be taken together since both have been held to display a Hibernicism in their use of *alius*. Binchy translates *ut detur ali indigenti* in Canon 5 'so that it may be given to some needy person' and says that this use of *alius* could only be explained in terms of the influence of Irish *alaile* which may mean 'a certain' as well as 'another'.[19] Bieler, very properly, objects that it is equally possible to take *alius* in its normal Latin sense.[20] The situation is that a collection has been made for someone in need. More has been contributed than is necessary. The balance is to be given to 'another person in need'.[21]

Having rightly argued against Binchy's case for the Hibernian use of *alius* in Canon 5, Bieler discovers what he believes is an instance of it in Canon 11:[22] *quicumque clericus ab aliquo excommonicatus fuerit et alius eum susciperit* . . . He argues that it would be pointless to emphasize that the person referred to by *alius* is different from the excommunicator and the excommunicated and holds that *alius* is here the same in meaning as *aliquis*. But there is surely no question of emphasizing the difference: *alius* simply brings a third party into the situation.[23] Classical Latin provides parallels: *ne mox victos victoresque defessos alius aggrederetur* 'for fear that within a short time a third power would attack conquered and conquerors, who were both worn out' (Sallust, *Iugurtha* 79, 4); *amicum qui non defendit alio culpante* 'a man who fails to stand up for his friend when another person (not another friend) finds fault with him' (Horace, *Satires* 1, 4, 82.). Neither Canon 5 nor Canon 11 displays a specifically Hibernian form of Latin.

Most recently, Bieler has discussed the use in the canons of *gentes, gentilis* and *homo gentilis* and has attempted to distinguish two strata, an early one, represented in Canons 13, 14 and 20, where *gentes* and *gentiles* bear the traditional meaning of 'pagans', and a later one, represented in Canons 8 and 24, where *(homo) gentilis* and *gentes*, by virtue of a peculiarly Irish innovation, mean 'lay-man' and 'lay-people'.[24] Previously, in his edition of the *Irish Penitentials*, Bieler had translated *gentilis (homo)* in Canon 8 as 'pagan': *clericus si pro gentili homine fideiusor fuerit in quacumque quantitate et si contigerit, quod mirum non †potest, per astutiam aliquam gentilis ille clerico fallat* . . . It is difficult to see what reason he has for changing his mind on this point. Not only does the translation 'pagan' create no intrinsic difficulty, but there is also in its favour the fact that a lack of trust in the reliability of *gentiles* such as seems to be indicated by *quod mirum non †potest*, is perhaps more likely to have been expressed about pagans than lay-members of the Church.[25] Canon 24 decrees that an intruding cleric is not to perform his sacred functions until he obtains permission from the bishop: *nam qui a gentibus sperat permissionem alienus sit*. A contrast between receiving permission from a bishop and receiving it from lay-people is not unattractive. Yet in a missionary situation what would be more natural than for an intruder to turn to some yet unconverted chieftain, with whom the local bishop would carry no weight, and get permission from him to set up his church? Bieler's present interpretation of *gentes* and *gentilis* in these two canons cannot be proved wrong. At the same time he has not brought forward any proof that these words are not to be translated by 'pagan' as in the rest of the document.

The conclusion to which this discussion leads is that none of the linguistic arguments so far advanced has positively established that the document as a whole, or even any individual canon, is post Patrician.

M.J. McGann

POSTSCRIPT

In *Studia Hibernica* 8 (1968), pp 49-59, Binchy has returned to the study of *The Bishops' Synod*. He still finds 'glaring difference in grammar and style between this document and Patrick's own writings', yet speaks at the same time of 'the technical language used in the decrees' (p 51). He now accepts Bieler's argument about Canon 5, but adheres to his view concerning *iurare ad*, noting Bieler's acceptance of it (p 51 and n 9).

M.J. McG.

NOTES

1. *Studia Hibernica* 2 (1962), pp 45-49.

2. *Mélanges Mohrmann*, pp 96-102; *Irish Ecclesiastical Record* (January - June 1967), pp 9f. See also 'St. Patrick and the Coming of Christianity', pp 16-18, 86-90.

3. *Op cit*, pp 46f.

4. *The Life and Legend of St. Patrick*, p 130 n 20; *The Works of St. Patrick*, p 13.

5. *Op cit*, p 47. His ironically intended comment on the first of them, 'whereupon, of course, Patrick proceeded to forget all about his 'models' and reverted to his own inimitable and ungrammatical Latin', presents a not implausible picture: with the change of genre, the 'models' are no longer relevant and may be 'forgotten'.

6. *Mélanges Mohrmann*, pp 97f.

7. *The Latin of Saint Patrick*, p 10.

8. 'St. Patrick and the Coming of Christianity', p 17. Bieler's edition of the *Penitentials* contains no example other than those in the *Synod*.

9. Cf D.S. Nerney, *Irish Ecclesiastical Record* 72 (1949), p 24.

10. *Op cit*, p 48.

11. *Mélanges Mohrmann*, pp 99-101; *Irish Ecclesiastical Record* 107, pp 9f.

12. *Op cit*, p 47.

13. *Mélanges Mohrmann*, p 101.

14. T, cols 246f.

15. Cf also *Ériu* 4, 134, 18.

16. I am grateful to Proinsias MacCana for helping me to clarify this point.

17. *Thesaurus Linguae Latinae* I, col 520.

18. Cf Terence, *Andria* 728.

19. *Op cit*, p 47.

20. *Mélanges Mohrmann*, p 100.

21. I am grateful to W.C. Kerr for pointing out an interesting parallel: *pius Edus solvit bovem de suo aratro, deditque illum indigenti . . . . simili modo cultrum suum sanctus Edus alii indigenti homini dedit.* (C. Plummer, *Vitae Sanctorum Hiberniae* I p 36).

22. *Mélanges Mohrmann*, p 101 and cf. n. 19 above.

23. On this view Bieler's conjecture *ob aliquod* (*Mélanges Mohrmann*, *loc cit*) is not called for.

24. *Irish Ecclesiastical Record*, *loc cit*.

25. *Irish Ecclesiastical Record*, *loc cit*.

PATRICIUS AUXILIUS ISSERNINUS

Well, I should like to be very short with your permission, because I feel we have got our guests who can make much more valuable contributions than I can. It seems to me that we must just look at the introduction with its references to Patrick, Auxilius and Isserninus. If one accepts that the document is Patrician, then one gets a fairly close dating – provided one accepts the chronicle dates for these three people. The interesting omission there, of course, is Secundinus. The order has generally been assumed to be chronological – Secundinus died before the others – but I would just like to throw out the idea that it could be geographical. If there is anything in the suggestion that a later age glossed the name Palladius as Patricius, I think I am right in saying that the probable missionary area of Palladius was the South, and Auxilius and Isserninus are associated with places south of the Liffey, whereas Secundinus is further to the north. There is, I think, a possibility to be explored that this is perhaps a document emanating from the Southern Irish church and taken over later for purposes of the Northern.

From the point of view of proper names which I was specially asked to look at, there is this phrase 'the Roman fashion', which Binchy has rather gone nap on as indicating a late date, with its possible reference to the controversy between the southern church, conforming to Roman practice more rapidly, and the northern, but I do not believe that such absolute validity is possible. It is indeed very likely, I think, that this is a canon which is found on the Continent and refers to Roman, in contrast to barbarian or Eastern, or something like that, instead of the classic Irish situation of Roman as opposed to Northern Irish. One of the references – I have not got time to go into them all – to proper names does suggest, of course, an early date. It comes to us from the corrupt *Britanis* of Canon 33 which Professor Bieler renders 'the Britons' but which could be 'the Britains'. This could suggest strongly a period when it was still generally recognised, or better still generally remembered, that in the Roman period, the Britains correspond to what we would call Britain, Roman Britain being, in fact, four provinces.

Archaeologically, the document was disappointing. I just want to mention one place where I do feel that, and I think Professor Bieler would agree, we were right to fault him – the place where in his rendering of Canon 1, he translated *quesierit* as 'collected money' (*Penitentials*, p (55)). Now there is nothing in the Latin to justify 'money'. If there had been a

28

reference to money here the document would have been — would have had to have been — later than any date which has been suggested: indeed, later than the actual manuscript; so it is a useful illustration of the need to keep one's eye on the Latin while one is running down a translation — much more hinged on the Latin, very obviously, than in many other cases. We were not bound to archaeological implications when we were discussing the translation of *ecclesia* though sometimes it was not clear whether it was the church in an institutional sense or the church in an architectural sense. There was a certain amount of discussion on the 'bishop's altar'. Is this the bishop's altar in a church, in a conglomeration of churches forming a monastic enclosure or confined to a monastic enclosure, or is it another word really for 'cathedral' where a bishop normally said his Mass? The problems which came out of the text do not only concern the length or cut of a tunic. There is the knotty question of the 'monk and maiden travelling' or should it be the 'monk and nun travelling together'. They travelled in a *currus* whatever that was, and they travelled from — and here we admittedly ducked — 'settlement to settlement', we being reluctant to give too particular a sense to the Latin *villa*. But I do not think one would get very far along these paths.

Essentially, I think the problem remains though I do think we can now see it rather more clearly. Is the work a late compilation heavily based on early material — my own feeling — or is it an early compilation with late interpolations? I think that is really the problem, and as I say, I would opine that it is a relatively late collection of archaic material. One thing I feel is quite clear is that this document is of no value whatever for the great problem of Irish history, the date of the Patrick who wrote the *Confession* and the *Epistle*.

R.H.M. Dolley

COMMENTARY

Introduction

praemonere culpare que facta — All later editors have followed Spelman in inserting *quam* and expanding *q*: to *quae*. This would seem to be justified by *Collectio Hibernensis* LXVI, 18, *Patricius dicit Satius est nobis neglegentes praemonere ne delicta abundent quam culpare quae sunt facta. Salomon melius est arguere quam irasci*, but only if one assumes that *Collectio Hibernensis* represents a better text from which our version has lost the words *ne delicta abundent quam*. We are inclined to think, however, that this and other discrepancies between our manuscript and *Collectio Hibernensis* are due rather to an attempt by the compiler of *Collectio Hibernensis* to make better Latin out of his original. We have, in the main, tried to avoid emendation as much as possible if any sense could be got from the text as it stands, and so have chosen to expand *q*: to *que*. A strict interpretation of Spelman's version would demand that what follows were warnings against situations which had not yet arisen, but if this is so, it is hard to understand the lack of any order in the advice and prohibitions and also the specific detail of some of the situations, eg Nos 8, 9, 16, and 22. Our version would rather suggest that what follows is a collection of answers given by various bishops (not necessarily only those named in the heading) to questions that arose in the early Irish Church, which at once censures what has been done and warns against such behaviour.

melius est arguere quam irasci — This is a non-Vulgate version of *Ecclesiasticus* 20, 1, where the Vulgate following the Greek has *quam bonum est*.

It is interesting that recent English versions of the Bible seem to have followed King James's translators in rendering the passage as if the text were something like our Latin: 'it is much better to reprove than to be angry secretly' (1611); 'how much better to rebuke than to fume' (Jerusalem Bible, 1969); 'how much better it is to complain than to nurse a grudge' (New English Bible, 1970).

CANON 1

In interpreting this canon, previous editors since Ware have used the apparently similar canon in *Collectio Hibernensis* XLII, 25c.

Si quis redemptionem captivi inquaesiverit suo iure sine permissione abbatis, meruit excomminicari.

eg Bieler (*Penitentials* p (55))

'If anyone has collected money for captives in his community on his own, and without permission, he has deserved to be excommunicated.'

While accepting that this canon probably refers to the same situation as do Nos 4, 5 and 32, we find the words *in questionem quesierit* difficult to translate (see *infra*). Bieler's 'collected money' must surely be rejected since money was not coined in Ireland before the Norse kingdom of Dublin. Previous editors also have referred these canons to the Church's generally accepted duty to ransom prisoners of war or those who, like Patrick himself, had been sold into slavery by raiders, cf Patrick *Epistle* 14 where Patrick reproaches Coroticus with conduct which is the exact opposite of the custom of the Roman Christian Gauls, who ransom baptised prisoners from the Franks and other heathen with many thousands of *solidi*. Some of us, however, were inclined to think that these canons should be referred rather to a situation under Irish law where a criminal or defaulting debtor might become the property of the injured party, eg the story of Libran in Adomnan, *Life of Columba* 87a, cf *infra* Canon 32.

In its version of this canon, the *Collectio Hibernensis* gives the abbot as author of the permission, while in its version of Canon 4, it gives the bishop as the authority. K. Hughes (p 125) reconciles the difficulty by assuming that a scribe of the *Collectio Hibernensis* has substituted the abbot in the first case for the bishop that originally stood there, without noticing what he had done, perhaps to conform to later usage. While we agree that our text must originally have stated who was to grant permission we did not accept that the word *pontificis* in Canon 5 was enough to justify Dr. Hughes' conjecture. It does however highlight the difficulty of trying to establish the archetype of our manuscript and the *Collectio Hibernensis*.

in questionem... quesierit − We have used the technical term 'questing' ie, asking for alms, to cover our difficulty in knowing whether here we have two words or three. We have not been able to find the form *inquaestio* and although the form *quaestio* does occur in a Scottish Council of 1225, the more common form is *quaestus* or *quaesta* which has given the French *quête*. In any case, regulations limiting the practice of making special collections in church are not common until the eleventh century, or later, after the rise of the mendicant orders.

CANON 2

lectores — The only instance in the Synod of a canon's being applied to a class of persons who are denoted by a plural noun.

denique — 'lastly'. The canon has been taken from another collection in which it held final place. Bieler's preferred explanation, that it is 'a mere particle of transition', is unsupported by the use of *denique* elsewhere. Besides, in this document, canons are not introduced by conjunctions with the exception of Canon 15. There, *et* binds closely together Canons 14 and 15, which are united also by the fact that they alone prescribe temporal penances. Bieler's other explanation " 'at long last' (implying previous admonitions to the same effect)" introduces a note of impatience which is out of place in the *genre*.

cognoscant . . . aecclesiam — The meaning is impossible to establish with precision. This does not justify Spelman's positing a *lacuna* after *cognoscant*. It is possible that the canon would be less obscure if it were known in its original context.

It is uncertain whether *aecclesiam* refers to the building, the congregation, or to both. Nor is it clear what kind of knowledge is required of the lector. Is he to find out to which *aecclesia* he has been assigned? Or is it a question of getting to know the customs, prejudices or enthusiasms of his congregation? The meaning, attested in Medieval Latin for *cognosco*, of 'recognise', 'acknowledge the rights of' seems unlikely: when *cognosco* is thus used, it takes as object words like *debita* which imply the existence of a claim.

psallat — For the lector's duties in this connexion, see the Spanish canon quoted by Villanueva *ad loc.*

The subjunctive is final.

vagus — Successive ecumenical and provincial councils of the early Church forbade clerics of any rank to leave the parish or diocese to which they had been ordained unless they received permission to do so: thus Canon 3 of the Council of Arles (314), Canon 16 of the Council of Nicaea (325), Canon 3 of the Council of Antioch (341), and Canon 5 of the Council of Chalcedon (451).

In view of this great weight of authority it was to be expected that the Irish Church would also seek to restrain its clerics from unauthorised movement to another parish or diocese. It is, perhaps, surprising that the Irish legislators should have used the apparently informal epithet *vagus* to describe the cleric who offended in this respect. The word is not used of clerics, so far as has been ascertained, in any of the canons of the fourth, fifth or sixth centuries, as the canons cited above illustrate. The nearest equivalent seems to be *ambulans*, eg Canon 15 of the Third Council of Orleans (538).

On the other hand, there is ample evidence of the use of *vagus* or *vagari* to describe a monk who left his monastery: cf. Basil of Caesarea (330-379), *Constitutiones* 8; Cassian (360-430), *De Institutis Coenobiorum* 10, 6; and Canon 19 of the First Council of Orleans (511) which deals with monks *qui fuerint pervagati.*

The question arises why the composer of our canon applied to his cleric an epithet which was normally, in those times (sixth century?), applied to monks. Was it just unfamiliarity with official ecclesiastical terminology or was he living at a time when most clerics were in fact monks?

Villanueva seems to have thought that *vagus* was used in our canon in the sense of leaving clerical duties for secular pursuits and quotes a canon of a council held at Carthage which he attributes to an Irish source: *Clericus per plateas et andronas certa et maxima sine officii sui necessitate non ambulet.* This is interesting because of the use in a literal sense of *ambulare*, which we have already seen used in other canons in an apparently technical sense. *Collectio Hibernensis* XXXIX, 11 confuses the issue by using both *vagus* and *ambulare* namely: *monachus inconsulto abbate vagus ambulans in plebe debet excommunicari.* Whether this canon has any connection with ours seems impossible to determine; if it has, it perhaps adds to the suspicion that our legislator is using *clericus* in the sense of *monachus.* In Chapter 66 of his *Regula*, Benedict requires that all necessities of a monastery, eg, water, garden and mill should be inside the monastery *ut non sit necessitas monachis evagandi*. In Appendix E of *The Wandering Scholars*, Helen Waddell lumps together the two senses of *vagus* ie, 'straying from the parish' and 'straying from clerical duties.'

in plebe — The obvious translation of *plebs* in this context is 'the community' ie, the local body of Christians. Here, however, again our legislator has used a word which is not usual in the canons of the councils; they speak of *parochia, ecclesia, civitas,* and our Canons 30 and 34 use *parruchia*. In the canon which we are now discussing, as in Canon 1 and elsewhere, our legislator could presumably have used *parruchia* if indeed he had in mind a parish. In the apparent absence of a Gaelic word derived from *plebs* like Welsh *plwyf,* it is possible only to conjecture what he had in mind. But if we are concerned here with a cleric in the generally accepted Western sense and with the universally applied ban on unauthorised movement from the parish of ordination, it is difficult to avoid the equation of *plebs* with 'parish' or whatever was the contemporary unit of ecclesiastical administration in Ireland. If, of course, our *clericus vagus* was a monk, a possibility we have hinted at above, it is possible that *plebs* should be taken to mean 'the monastic community'.

It should be remarked that the terse unconditional terms of Canon 3 seem at some variance with 33 and 34, which, if they are of the same context as Canon 3, do not exclude the strange cleric from the *plebs,* but merely debar him from clerical functions.

CANONS 4 AND 5

Although these are set out as separate canons in the manuscript, it is clear that they must be taken together, since the subject of *ponat* in Canon 5 must be supplied from *quis* in Canon 4. Further, *Collectio Hibernensis* XLII, 26, attributes to Patrick the following:

Si quis acceperit permissionem pontificis, et collectum sit pretium captivi, non plus exigat quam necessitas poscit. Si quid supra manserit, ponat super altare, et indigentibus detur et captivis.

Again, it is only from the *Collectio Hibernensis* version that we can assume that these canons refer to the ransoming of captives. The word *captivus* appears twice in the *Collectio Hibernensis* version, but does not appear at all in Canons 4 and 5 of *The Bishops' Synod*.

pontificis – This word occurs in the first sentence of the *Collectio Hibernensis* version and in the second sentence of our version. Two points seem to need discussion here:

> (a) Is there anything unusual in the use of the word *pontifex* rather than *episcopus* for 'bishop'?

> (b) Is *pontifex* ever used in an Irish context for 'abbot'? Is, in fact, the person mentioned in both 4 and 5 an abbot?

(a) In answer to (a) we can say that the two terms *pontifex* and *episcopus* were both used for bishop from an early period. *Pontifex* is found as early as Jerome, *Epistles* 108,6 while the noun *pontificatus* is used by Augustine, *Sermon* 340,2 (ed Diehl). Christine Mohrmann, remarking on the flexibility of the terminology of Christian Latin, says (*Etudes sur le latin des Chrétiens* II,104): 'Le terme technique *episcopus* fera place non seulement à *sacerdos*, qui était très usuel chez les chrétiens des premiers siècles, mais aussi à *pontifex* et à *antistes*, toutes deux expressions très romaines et très officielles.' In Merovingian Gaul *pontifex* seems actually to have been more usual than *episcopus*. Thus in the index to Levison's edition of Gregory of Tours, *pontifex* = *episcopus* appears forty times, *episcopus* on only ten occasions. The other writers whose work is published in the *MGH Scriptorum Rerum Merovingiarum* series also use *pontifex* extensively, though not so much so as Gregory: Baxter and Johnson cite occasional examples of its use from the seventh to the fifteenth centuries. One has the impression that the other meaning of 'supreme pontiff', ie, pope, which the word had from equally early times, gained ground at the expense of the meaning 'bishop' throughout the early Middle Ages. The words derived from *pontifex* – *pontificatus*, *pontificalis* survived also, and, in fact, *pontificalia* is the only and usual word even in the high Middle Ages for the regalia and vestments of a bishop. However, the Hiberno-Latin writers do not seem to use *pontifex*. It does not occur in either of Adomnan's works or in Columbanus.

(b) There do not seem to be any cases of *pontifex* = *abbas* either in the other *Penitentials* or in the above-mentioned, which are the only Hiberno-Latin works of the 'monastic period' with adequate indexes. *Episcopus* is used at least once in Adomnan for the abbot of Cul-Rathin (Coleraine) who was also a bishop (*Life of Columba*, p 319).

What is offered as a contribution to the collection made in Canon 4? Money is ruled out. Cattle are the monetary standard, but obviously could not be used in this case. The *pretium* of 4 would be reckoned in cattle and paid for by other more easily-handled objects, such as ornaments, rings and trinkets. Contributions to the redemption of captives would be made in the form of these. If these proved to be of a value greater than the *pretium* required, there might be a surplus which could not easily be given back to the original donors. This, then, would explain the *Si quid supra manserit* of Canon 5. In this connexion, it is interesting to note Patrick. *Confessio* 49 ... *mulieribus religiosis quae mihi ultronea munuscula donabant et super altare iactabant ex ornamentis suis et iterum reddebam illis et adversuo me scandalizabantur.* Perhaps the incident in the *Vita Columbae* cited above, where Conall the abbot-bishop of Coleraine collected *pene innumerabilia xenia* from the local inhabitants and had them blessed by St Columba, is a survival of an earlier custom into the 'monastic period'. But the gifts there were to be used in alms-giving. There is no mention of redeeming captives.

The phrase *altare pontificis* is odd in that Irish churches of this period were extremely small for the most part, and one can more easily imagine a plurality of churches than of altars.

ali – Probably a case of haplography for *alii*. The correct spelling, *alii*, together with the following *indigenti* would involve the scribe in five successive down-strokes, so that the omission of one is easily understood. In Hiberno-Latin texts *alius* is sometimes used with the meaning of Old Irish *alaile* 'a certain' (cf Adomnan's *Life of Columba*, p 584; Bieler, *Penitentials*, p 37). However, there seems no reason why this should be so here. The two translations – 'to another needy person', or 'to a needy person' – are not, in any case, very different. On this point Bieler himself says, *loc cit*, note 1 'In Pa I. 5 . . . . the pronoun might have its normal meaning'.

CANON 6

The scribe of our manuscript has again set this out as two separate canons, with a capital E at *Et uxor.* Another manuscript from Corpus Christi College, Cambridge, No 265, p 104, appears to have a version of this canon, but with *corporis* in place of *ventris*, and ending with the words, *et si non more Romano capillos et barbam tonderit, excommunicetur.*

Wasserschleben, in his edition of the *Collectio Hibernensis*, p 213, records that his manuscript No 6, the *Valicellanus*, has the whole canon, but he prints only *Patricius*.

Si quis clericus cuius capilli non sunt tonsi more Romano debet excommunicare.

It is clear from the position of this citation in the *Collectio* that the compiler was citing it in connexion with the seventh-century controversy about the shape of the tonsure. Some later editors have also taken this view, eg, Haddan and Stubbs. Although it is attractive in that it would give a seventh-century date for this canon, we have rejected it in favour of the idea that what is being commended is a short haircut after the Roman fashion. Some light may be thrown on this by the Welsh canon mentioned by K. Hughes p 48 (*Synodus Wallica* A6.1; Bieler, *Penitentials*, p 48), which requires that no catholic shall let his hair grow *more barbarorum*. Bieler (*op cit*, p 7), following Haddan and Stubbs' dating of the Welsh Synod to between 550 and 650, associates this document with Brittany, and thinks that the title *Excerpta de Libris Romanorum et Frankorum* refers to the Roman Britons who settled in Brittany and their Frankish overlords. That long hair was the mark of the Frankish nobility is clear from the grim tale of the fate of the sons of Chlodomir in Gregory of Tours, *History of the Franks* 3, 18. There, too, short hair is not so much the distinguishing mark of the clergy as of *reliqua plebs* ie of non-Franks.

It is hard to believe that the pious Queen Clothilde would have preferred to see her grandsons dead rather than priested — *mortuos quam tonsos* — though Gregory does remark that she was so distracted with terror as not to know what she was saying; then he adds to the confusion by describing how a third son (he has given his name to the Paris suburb of St Cloud) escaped, and *sibi manu propria capillos incidens clericus factus est. More Romano*, in our canon then, would only mean 'in Roman fashion' and not necessarily a tonsure of any special shape.

tunica — The problem is to transpose the classical Roman *tunica*, the garment worn under the toga but over everything else, ordinarily of knee-length, to Ireland in the Dark Ages. The canon speaks of going without such a garment, and thus exposing the *venter* (= stomach, from other references in Bieler's *Penitentials*) and being, at least in part, naked. The looping of a garment over the belt for greater freedom of movement does not seem to meet the case.

The suggestion that *tunica* is some equivalent of the modern soutane is probably correct; ie, the canon forbids clergy to walk out out of uniform. This inference is supported by Vulgate use of *tunica* as priestly dress, notably, *Leviticus* 6, 10; 16, 4; also by parallels cited by Villanueva. (For what it is worth, thirteenth-century English canons emphasise that clerical dress should be fastened (*cappis clausis et indumentis honestis utantur*) and associate rules for clerical dress with rules for the tonsure, cf *Councils and Synods*, ed Powicke and Cheney, pt 1, 26, 63, 407, 429.) Whether Villanueva is justified in his further suggestion that the clergy are being forbidden native dress is more doubtful.

uxor – We were not on the whole convinced by Dr Hughes' suggestion that the use of this word instead of Vinnian's and Columbanus' *clentela* implied an earlier date for our canon, before the word *clentella* had come into ordinary use. In the instances cited from these penitentials, the cleric's spouse has usually done something more disgraceful than going about with her head uncovered, and so may be thought to deserve a harsher name.

ab ecclesia separentur – Both the *Collectio Hibernensis* and the other Cambridge manuscript said to be of the tenth or eleventh century replace this phrase with the verb *excommunicari* which, we suppose, is what the phrase means.

CANON 7

ussus neglegentiae causa – *ussus* presents difficulty. One possible emendation would be *iussus* as implied in Bieler's translation though not otherwise indicated by him. A literal translation, however, raises the question of the source and context of such an order. If, on the other hand, this is a form of *usus* (which is also implied by Bieler's translation) this may be due to a common Hibernicism ('*ss*' for '*s*') or to a possible error through the recurrent letters in *clericus usus, cf* Canon 25. On this assumption, *ussus* would be either the participle governing *causa*, giving the unsatisfactory meaning 'using the pretext of negligence' or the noun, genitive: 'because of indifference to custom'.

ad collectas – Possibly either 'collects', ie prayers, or 'assembly'.

mane uel uespere – Though these were emerging as public hours of worship, the translation 'matins' and 'vespers' would appear an anachronistic interpretation.

occurrerit – The verb *eo* tends to be replaced by such circumlocutions.

nisi forte – Possibly a stock formula = *nisi*; or *forte*, if meaning 'perhaps', implies a loop-hole which is unlikely; 'happen' might be preferable.

iugo servitutis – Slavery, if literal, cf Bieler, *Penitentials*, Columbanus B20, p 104, line 12 *de servitutis iugo*, of freeing an *ancilla* (a word often used theologically in a non-literal sense). Against this, it seems unlikely that a cleric would be made a *servus*. This might be true of the earliest period of Christianity in Ireland, when a Christian could have been taken into captivity by a non-Christian raiding party. It surely cannot be true of the 'monastic' period, when the cleric counted as a member of the privileged class of *filidh*. Also, the suddenness of his being taken into slavery, as implied in this text, seems odd. It sounds as if he was envisaged as being present at one service and then suddenly being made a *servus* before he could attend the next.

If the meaning is not literal, perhaps it could refer to the routine work in the monastery. But there does not seem to be any evidence that in the Celtic monastery necessary manual work was done in rotation, and that those whose turn it was to do this work were excused attendance at services. On the contrary, from Adomnan, *Vita Columbae*, we have the impression that each person had a job permanently assigned to him: eg, a cook at Iona (3,10); a *pincerna* (1, 17); and a group of *operarii fratres* referred to as building a wall (3,23). This permanent assignment of jobs would be more in keeping with the Irish social structure than a rotation of jobs, which might mean that a member of a noble family would have to do menial work. It is significant that neither Columba, nor his relative Baithene, ever seem to take a turn at manual work, but concentrate on teaching and copying books.

It has also been suggested that the phrase could refer to a slave turned cleric.

CANON 8

In the manuscript there is a mark of punctuation after *quantitate, rebus suis, debitum*. After the last, *Nam* occurs with a capital. However, as the punctuation is nowhere regular, these marks are probably of little significance.

gentili – This may mean

    (a)   pagan (cf titulus 31 of the *Second Synod of St Patrick*)

    (b)   kinsman

(a) In Western Europe at this time the usual word for pagan was *paganus* (fifth to seventh centuries). In spite of this, the use of *a gentibus* in Canon 13 lends support to this meaning for *gentilis* here. *Gentes* later gave rise to an Irish word applied to Norsemen.

(b) Kinsman or member of the *gens*. This is, perhaps, the more obvious meaning, and appears, though with some reservations, in the suggested translation below.

fideiusor – According to Professor Binchy in *Studia Hibernica* 8, suretyship was of three types, in which the guarantor stood surety

(a) with his property;

(b) with his person ie, he became a hostage till the principal satisfied the debt;

(c) with his authority and honour, guaranteeing that the principal would fulfil his obligations.

There was no state enforcement, but the guarantor of category (c) had the right even to kill a defaulter for the slight to his honour. In this case, too, the guarantor had to be of higher social status than the person for whom he stood surety, and must, therefore, be a member of the noble ranks. Clerics were not eligible in the fifth century but became eligible in the sixth.

fuerit – The question again arises of whether this is future perfect indicative or perfect subjunctive.

quantitate – *quantitas* usually means a sum of money.

contigerit – cf *fuerit* above.

CANON 9

This canon clearly demands a monastic setting. Indeed, it looks like an abbot's ruling on the conduct required of his monks, yet the omission of any mention of a sanction places it in a different category from the penitentials of Columbanus or Vinnian. That there were monks and *virgines Christi* in Patrick's Church is clear from *Confessio* 41, but the prohibitions in this canon seem unsuited to a missionary situation. Certainly writers of the Later Middle Ages seem to have thought that Patrick's Church was less strict in segregating the sexes than was the later church, cf the well-known passage in the *Catalogus*, while the *Life of Monenna* by Conchubranus, ch 5 (eleventh century) sends Monenna and her companions travelling across Ireland to Bishop Iban for instruction.

curru, villa — The use of these words suggested to some of us that this might be a canon borrowed from the Continent, perhaps from Merovingian France. But Columba in Ireland travels in a *currus* which has room for his driver as well (Adomnan, *Vita Columbae* 90A).

We have not found so early a use of *villa* in an Irish setting. Patrick's father's *villa* or *villula* in *Confessio* 1 was not in Ireland. But again we find the word in later hagiographers meaning 'settlement' or 'farm' (eg, Conchubranus, *Monenna* ch 6; Anonymous, *Vita S. Carthagi*, ch 33). In short, we think that this canon probably comes from the developed Irish Church of the sixth century. It may have been included here because it was issued by an abbot who was also a bishop, eg Conall of Coleraine, (Adomnan, *Vita Columbae* 5A). Villanueva, pp 42-57, has a long *excursus* — a history of monasticism both Irish and foreign.

CANON 10

The subject of this canon is not named. It may come from the same source as Canon 2 and refer to the duties of the lector. Since the recitation of the psalter, however, was so much part of the discipline of a monastery, we are inclined to refer this to the same source as Canon 9.

comam habeat — Has a full head of hair. We get no help here in trying to determine what shape of tonsure, if any, was in vogue. We can find no good reason for the varying moods and tenses of the verbs.

CANON 11

After *utantur* there is a space and then an erasure apparently of two letters and a superscript stroke. The first letter seems to be '*c*', the second '*n*' or '*o*'.

Cf *Collectio Hibernensis* XXXIX, 10: (*De eo, quod ambo excommunicandi sunt, monachus fugitivus est* (sic: *et*) *susceptor illius*)*B. Patricius: quicunque excommunicatus fuerit a quolibet clericus, et ab alio susceptus fuerit, coaequali penitentia corripiantur.*

Bieler (Mélanges Mohrmann, p 101, n 19) finds difficulties in the text of Canon 11:

(a)   'The vague *ab aliquo*'. He suggests reading *ob aliquod*, comparing

41

Canon Hibernensis IV (9), *aliquod* (*-quid* B) *in eos committere.*

(b) '*Alius* could, of course, mean 'another cleric', but it is far more probable that the prohibition extends to all Christians (cf also such seventh-century canons as Cummean IX,2; *Synodus* II, c 4). Whichever may be the case, there was no point in emphasizing that the person referred to by *alius* would be different from the excommunicator and the excommunicated. I suggest . . . . to take *alius* to mean *aliquis*'. (Bieler, *Penitentials*, p 37, suggests influence of Irish *alaile*; cf Binchy, *Studia Hibernica* 2, on *ali* in c 5). Bieler adds that *alius* might be a fossil deriving from *Concilium Nicaense* c 5, *qui ab aliis* (namely, *episcopis*) *eiecti sunt non esse ab aliis admittendos*. 'However, the cases contemplated seem to be different.'

Neither point is free from objection. (a) *ob aliquod* is as vague as *ab aliquo*, and the suggested parallel is not one: *ea que sunt regis vel episcopi aut scribae furari aut rapere aut aliquod in eos committere*, translated by Bieler 'or to commit any (other crime) against them.' (b) Of the two canons cited in support of taking *alius* to mean 'any Christian', Cummean (quoted below' in discussion of *susciperit*) may be relevant, *Synodus* II almost certainly is not: *repellis excommunicatum a communione et mensa et missa et pace*. A decision in the present case is closely bound up with the meaning of *susciperit*. It seems perfectly natural that the author, having to introduce a third person into the situation, should choose *alius*. There seems to be no good reason for accepting either Bieler's conjecture or his interpretation of *alius*.

susciperit – Used both of 'taking in' strangers (Vinneanus 33) and of 'taking back' an erring wife (Vinneanus 42-5). The apparent severity of the penance imposed on *alius* (see below on *coaequali*) would indicate that he has done a great deal more than give hospitality to the excommunicated cleric (contrast Cummean IX, 2: *qui communi-caverit non ignorans ab ecclesia excommunicato, xl peniteat*, under the rubric *DE MINUTIS CAUSIS*).

coaequali – Is not unambiguous. It is most likely to mean that by his action *alius* has made himself liable to the same *penitentia* as is necessary for the restoration of the excommunicated cleric to full membership of the church (cf Canon 18).

utantur – *uti* in itself does not seem suspect. But the erasure raises questions, and *Collectio Hibernensis* gives no support. *covertantur* (ABS) might be considered, cf Vinneanus 44, *si forte conversa fuerit ad penitentiam*. It does not seem possible to make anything out of *commutantur*.

CANON 12

There seems little difficulty in establishing the general sense of this canon, namely, that alms are not to be accepted from an excommunicated Christian. A number of points arise, however, which require comment:

1. **Orthography**

   (a) *excominicatus* (Lewis and Short *excommunicatus*)

Elsewhere in our manuscript this and cognate words are invariably spelt with the central element *'common'*. The omission in this canon of *'m'* and the substitution of *'i'* for *'o'*, if they are due to anything other than carelessness in transmission, might perhaps have taken place because an ignorant scribe was writing down the canon from dictation by a person whose pronunciation was not above reproach. The colloquial form of the canon might be thought to reinforce this suggestion.

   (b) *elimosina* (Lewis and Short *eleemosyna*)

This spelling, which is repeated in Canon 13, is one of several variants used in the *Irish Penitentials*, eg, *elymosina* (Vinneanus), *helemosina* (Columbanus), *aelimosina* (*Canones Wallici* A). Clearly, there was widespread uncertainty about the correct spelling of this Greek word; it is, perhaps, significant that our spelling is found on a coin of Pippin, the father of Charlemagne (M. Prou, *Les Monnaies Carolingiennes*, p II).

2. **Comparison with Collectio Hibernensis**

An apparently related canon in *Collectio Hibernensis* (XL, 8), as given by Wasserschleben, reads: *Quicunque clericus excommunicatus fuerit, nec ejus elemosina in ecclesia recipiatur.*

   (a) *clericus*

The application of the principle to all Christians made in our canon would seem to imply that the canon was formulated at a time when stricter views were held on this matter than at the time when the parallel canon in *Collectio Hibernensis* was formulated. It is interesting to speculate whether the stricter view is the earlier or the later; if more evidence were available about the attitude of the early Irish Church at different periods, it might help to determine the temporal relationship between our canons and *Collectio Hibernensis*.

   (b) *in ecclesia*

The inclusion of the expression *in ecclesiam* in our Canon 13, which seems to be deliberately juxtaposed to Canon 12, gives rise to the conjecture that the expression has perhaps been accidentally omitted from Canon 12; but it can be no more than a conjecture.

3. **nec**

Bieler, copiously supported by Lewis and Short, translates *nec* as 'not even'. This gives a nice contrast to the use of the simple *non* in Canon 13, where there is of course no question of admitting a pagan into church fellowship.

It may be remarked, however, that the use of *nec* as a simple negative is attested, eg, Virgil, *Eclogue* 9, 6;

Nunc victi tristes, quoniam Fors omnia versat,
Hos illi (quod nec vertat male) mittimus haedos.

It is suggested, therefore, that the possibility should not be excluded that *nec* here simply means 'not'.

CANON 13

offerendam — A passive adjective, implying neither obligation nor completeness.

in ecclesiam — literal or conceptual? Probably literal. Pagans did sometimes offer alms — a kind of half-way stage to conversion. It was permissible to use these but not to collect them actually in the church.

CANON 14

Cf *Collectio Hibernensis, XXVIII, 10:*

Qui occiderit aut fornicationem fecerit aut more gentilium aruspicem interrogaverit, per singula cremina annum penitentiam agat, et illo impleto cum testibus postea resolvetur a sacerdote.

ad aruspicem iuraverit — We have not accepted Binchy's suggestion in *Studia Hibernica* 8 that this is inspired by the Gaelic idiom *tonguid do,* cf p 24. We also avoid Bieler's loaded translation of 'Druid'. Muirchu, *Vita Patricii* I, 9, mentions *aurispices* as present at the court of Loegaire, and again in I, 14 (*auruspicibus*) which may be meant to represent the same Irish word. *Aruspex* occurs several times in the Vulgate with the meaning soothsayers, eg in *Daniel* 2, 27, where it is used of those who were unable to interpret Nebuchadnezzar's dream. What is surprising is that, while the other major sins of murder and fornication are named, idolatry is represented here by swearing before a soothsayer (consulting a soothsayer,*Collectio Hibernensis*) and in Canon 16, by believing in a *lamia. Collectio Hibernensis* attributes No 14, but not 16, to Patricius but it seems unlikely that the Patrick of the *Confessio* would not have had to deal with more, and more serious survivals from paganism.

sacerdote — Where this word occurred already in Canon 6, we translated it 'bishop', relying mainly on the views of Professor Mohrmann cited in our notes to Canon 5. In the present case we doubted if reconciliation belonged exclusively to the bishop. Bieler's *Penitentials sv sacerdos* show several examples of this word in connection with penance, where the same doubt arises. In one case in Columbanus B, canon 4, p 100, *sacerdos* seems to be distinguished from *episcopus*.

CANON 15

Cf *Collectio Hibernensis XXIX, 8:*

Qui furtum fecerit dimidium annum peniteat, XX diebus cum pane et aqua vivat, et rapta restituat, si fieri potest, et sic in ecclesia recipiatur.

demedium — Sc *annum* as in the *Collectio Hibernensis* version.

repraesentet — The meaning 'to pay out money on completion of an agreement' is sufficiently attested in classical Latin. Here we seem to have the prefix *re* being used to mean 'pay back'.

renuetur — Bieler's suggested gloss *renovetur* would be more acceptable if, like *Collectio Hibernensis*, our manuscript had *ecclesia* instead of *ecclesiam*. The accusative can be taken either in the material or conceptual sense of the church, the ablative more probably in the material sense only.

CANON 16

lamiam in saeculo, quae interpraetatur striga – Three points arise here:

(a)   Do either of these words refer only to vampires, or to witches in general? In classical Latin *lamia* could have both meanings. The *lamia* of Horace,*Ars Poetica* 340: *neu pransae Lamiae vivum puerum extrahat alvo*, is surely a vampire. But the more general use of the word seems to be a witch, cf Apuleius,*Metamorphosis* 1, 83: *lamiae illae*. Tertullian, *Adversus Valentinianos* 3, has *lamiae terrores* referring to imaginary monsters used by nurses to frighten children. In the medieval period, we have a clear reference to vampires in Gervase of Tilbury's *Otia Imperialia* 3, 87: *Lam(i)ae dicuntur esse mulieres quae .... infantes ex cunis extrahunt.* This word was used by Jerome to translate the Hebrew *Lilith* – a she-devil (*Isaiah* 34, 14 : *ibi cubavit lamia et invenit suam requiem*) and it may be that its use as a general term for a demon here led to a similar use as a general term by medieval writers, who are more likely to have been familiar with this passage than any other. Curiously enough, the Authorized Version translated *lamia* as 'screech owl', a clear confusion with *strix*.

strix/striga is found as a vampire in Ovid, *Fasti* 4, 135: *nocte volant, puerosque petunt nutricis egentes* and in Petronius, *Satyricon* 63, 8: *scilicet iam puerum strigae involaverant.* Petronius is the first writer to use the form *striga* formed by analogy on *strix* which all medieval writers use and which must have been the form preferred in the spoken language as it has survived in Romance.

- Festus defines the *strigae* in very general terms as *maleficae mulieres* and *volaticae* (ed Lindsay, p 414).

striga clearly means 'vampire' in Charlemagne's *Capitulare Saxonicum* (ed *M.G.H. Leges* II, p 68, s 6): *Si quis a diabulo deceptus crediderit virum aliquem vel feminam strigam esse et homines commedere ... capitali sententia punietur*; in the first Lombard laws, the Edict of Rothar(AD 643) (s 179, ed Muratori, *Rerum Italicarum Scriptores* I, ii, p 47C): *Nullus praesumat aldiam alienam aut ancillam quasi strigam, quae dicitur masca occiderit, quia Christianis mentibus nullatenus est credendum, nec possible est, ut hominem mulier vivum intrinsecus possit commedere*; and in the *Lex Salica* (tit LXVII, ch iii)) *Si stria hominem comederit, et convicta fuerit.* An earlier reference in the Edict of Rothar (s 197, p 31 A): *Si quis mundiam de puella libera aut muliere habens, eam strigam quod est masca clamaverit* ... does not specify what the *striga*'s crime is. So the medieval Latin references seem to favour the meaning of 'vampire'. On the other hand, in the Romance languages, the words derived from *striga* are translated as 'witch' in the dictionaries.

According to Montague Summers in *The Vampire: his Kith and Kin*, many witches were held to have the same blood-sucking habits as vampires, and the distinction between the two is very hard to draw. But it seems logical to suppose that the words *striga* and *lamia* are exact synonyms here.

(b) The comparative rarity of *lamia* as opposed to *striga* seems to account for the *quae interpraetatur*. Note that Gervase of Tilbury also seems to feel the need for some explanation − *dicuntur esse. lamia* is found hardly at all in the Romance languages. Meyer-Lubke, *Romanisches Etymologisches Wörterbuch*, records it only in the dialect of Lucca, and as a borrowing in Basque. *striga* on the other hand, gives standard Italian *strega*; north Italian *striga, stria*; Rumanian *striga*; Old French *estrie*; Portuguese *estria*. An alternative explanation is that the word *lamia* is not known in Ireland whereas *striga* is. Unfortunately, I have not been able to find out anything regarding the belief in vampires in Irish folklore. (Summers does not deal with Ireland in his book, but says in his preface that he will deal with Irish vampires in a sequel − *The Vampire in Europe*.) But the similarity between Canon 16 and the Edict of Rothar is striking. Both insist that it is the belief in the existence of a vampire that is wrong. One wonders whether this canon goes back to Germanic (Frankish?) source.

(c) Finally, there seems to be no evidence anywhere for any connection between the *lamia/striga* and mirrors which would support Spelman's emendation of the manuscript *saeculo* to *speculo*.

anathemazandus − We agree with Bieler that it is a conflation of *anathemandus* and *anathematizandus*. No form *anathemazo* is found in the Thesaurus. Both the other forms are found frequently from patristic authors onwards.

As the sentence stands, *quicumque* ... *inposuerit* must be regarded as explanatory parenthesis. The alternative is to place a stop after *anathemazandus*. There is a mark in the manuscript after that word which could be for punctuation. The *nec* would have to be taken as co-ordinate with the following *et*. The passage would then translate: 'Whosoever has put that imputation upon a living soul is not to be received into the church before he retracts verbally the accusation he has made and so does penance with all diligence.' This would seem to make the *sic* redundant.

ante .. quam ut — No classical instance of *ante . . . quam ut* is recorded in Lewis and Short, but there is one example of *prius quam ut*, significantly in the 'colloquial' Cicero, *Epistulae ad Atticum* 4,1,1: *nihil prius mihi faciendum putavi quam ut*. It therefore does not seem impossible for *ut* to be used in this way in later Latin.

idem creminis — This use of the partitive genitive where there is really no partitive meaning is found in classical authors, though there it seems usually to have some special, though non-partitive meaning (see Ernout-Thomas, *Syntaxe Latine*, 2nd ed 1964, p 49, s 63b; Woodcock, *New Latin Syntax*, p 59, s 77ii). One would not expect to find it in late Latin, where even the more normal forms of partitive genitive were being replaced by *de* and ablative (see Ernout — Thomas, *op. cit.* p 47; Lofstedt, *Philologischer Kommentar zur Peregrinatio Aetheriae*, pp 106-9). But, on the other hand, Plautus is very fond of this same usage (cf *hoc negotii*, *Trinummus* 578, *Miles* 956; *hoc operis*, *Aulularia* 370; many further examples are in Lindsay, *Syntax of Plautus*, p 16), so that it may have existed in popular speech alongside the *de* and ablative construction, and this may explain its continued use in late Latin. The general impression one has is that partitive genitives are not at all common in late Latin. Yet there are several examples listed by Bieler from the *Penitentials* (*index grammaticus*, p 345, under heading *Nominis cum pronomine structura*).

iterum ... revocat — Pleonasm typical of later Latin usage. The manuscript originally read *revocet; cat* has been written above (by the same hand?). Bieler (p 39) suggests that *revocat* is really a subjunctive which has been assimilated to *agat*, because of a desire in the mind of the writer or scribe to rationalize the two case-endings. He gives many other examples of this *Reimzwang*, mostly from Hiberno-Latin, in *Classica et Mediaevalia* 15 (1954), pp 120-3.

The penance for this false accusation, which seems to consist merely in taking back the charge made, is extremely (and uncharacteristically?) light.

Virgo — We have rendered *virgo* as unmarried woman rather than nun since the situation in this canon, but not necessarily in No 9, seems to be not so much that of a woman in a religious community, but of one who has made a vow of chastity or continence, cf Patrick, *Confessio* 42, and Bieler, *Penitentials*, p 223. We have, therefore, taken *domus* as 'dwelling' not 'religious house', and *villa* as 'settlement' not 'religious community'.

permanet — Wilkins resolves the difficulty by emending *permanere*. The sixteenth-century transcription made for Archbishop Parker has *permaneat*. This would assume an ellipsis of either *quae* or *si* after *et*.

dimiserit adulterium — *dimittere* with an abstract object seems well enough attested, eg Suetonius, *Gaius 25, matrimonia dimiserit*, to justify the retention of the manuscript *adulterium* (gives up her adultery) in preference to the emendation *adulterum* (dismisses the adulterer).

CANON 18

nocte Pascharum — The eve of Easter day. The plural is unusual even for this word which varies in gender from neuter to feminine and, in Bede, to first declension masculine. Adomnan, *Vita Columbae*, p 60a, has *usque ad pascalium consummationem dierum* which is variously interpreted by his editors as Low Sunday or Whitsuntide.

Villanueva on the *Second Synod of St Patrick,* Canon 13, *In nocte Paschae fas est foras ferre*, points out that, as the text stands, these two canons cancel each other. If the Sacrament may be taken out of doors, then there is little point in barring the excommunicate from the church. He further notes that in the early church, the excommunicate was usually admitted to catechism, lesson and sermon, but he seems to have overlooked the fact that we have here an impenitent excommunicate. This may, indeed, give some indication of the date of our text. This is not a missionary situation. The church is well enough established for the notion of occasional conformity to be current, but the church is not yet so strong that an impenitent excommunicate will not try to defy its ban, ie our text is post-Patrician.

primo – This is an unexpected usage for *illo*. It may be this that has led Spelman and later editors to expect an object with *se iungere* and has made them emend *adulteriis* to *adultero*. In fact, the text, as it stands, makes reasonable sense: 'couples herself in adultery'.

haec – The plural may imply that two acts are involved, the desertion of the first husband, as well as the adultery.

CANON 20

Collectio Hibernensis XXX, le headed *Sinodus Romana* has:

Omnis qui fraudat debitum fratris ritu gentilium excommunis sit donec reddiderit.

cuiuslibet – *Collectio Hibernensis* has *fratris*, which seems to suggest that this is to be taken with *debitum* 'a debt owed to a brother; a debt owed to someone' rather than with *ritu gentilium* as Bieler's translation seems to imply. He has 'A Christian who acting like a Pagan fails to pay a debt', but it seemed to us that *ritu gentilium* should also be taken with *debitum*: 'a debt according to pagan custom', that is, a debt arising out of a transaction following native usage.

Our manuscript would then have a more extensive prohibition than *Collectio Hibernensis*. In the *Collectio Hibernensis* version, no-one may defraud a fellow Christian by using native law. In our version, a Christian may not defraud anyone by using native rather than Christian law. That is, Christians are bound by their obligations under civil law. This would agree with Columba's ruling in the story of Libran, in Adomnan, *Vita Columbae* 87ff.

CANON 21

dereliquerit – The verb *derelinquere* can be found with the meaning 'abandon', 'bequeath' or 'omit'. With the dative *cui* the meaning 'bequeath' would seem to make some sense, but one would expect also a direct object, which cannot be supplied. Bieler is probably right in suggesting that it has been used in mistake for *deliquerit*. Examples of this verb with the dative can be found in the Vulgate,

Jeremiah, 33, 8, and in the *Vetus Latina, Numbers* 5, 7 and *Psalm* 50, 6, where in both cases the Vulgate has *peccare.*

provocat eum – We have taken the subject to be *Christianus,* and the word *eum* to refer to the same person as *aliquis,* but if our conjecture *in duellum* were accepted, the subject might well be *aliquis,* and *eum* refer to *Christianus.*

imductum (manuscript); *in iudicium* (Spelman); *in duellum* (Dolley) – Spelman's emendation has found favour with all subsequent editors, but it has far-reaching implications in seeming to demand that all cases of tort involving a Christian should be heard by an ecclesiastical court. It would also weaken the probability of our interpretation of Canon 20, which seemed to hold that native custom was to be respected. Professor Dolley has suggested *in duellum,* which is no further from the *ductus litterarum* than *in iudicium,* goes very naturally with *provocat,* and while it does not involve an explicit rejection of the civil courts, does reject the manifestly un-Christian notion of settling a dispute by fighting. We would venture to translate it 'offers to fight him', without implying any notion of trial by combat. For *duellum* with the meaning of single combat see however Villanueva on Canon 8.

CANON 22

amaverit – The subject of this must be *filia.* The use of the word 'love' is surprising. A similar situation in Canon 19 is called adultery. It may be that the father's consent made the affair respectable by native convention.

dotem – This can hardly be a dowry, a settlement made by the father on the daughter, but rather a bride price, a payment by the bridegroom to the bride's kin.

CANON 23

presbiterorum – Both here and in Canon 32, the question arises of how much attention we are to pay to the partitive genitive. In Canons 28 and 29 *clericorum* and *fratrum* seem to be true partitives: 'any of the clerics', 'any of the brothers of a given community'. Here, however, it seems hard to make much distinction between 'if any of the priests' and 'if any priest'.

offerat — This word is taken to mean 'offer Mass', cf Gaelic *aifreann* from Latin *offerenda*.

CANON 24

Cf *Collectio Hibernensis XLIII, 4:*

Si quis advena ingressus fuerit in plebem, non ante baptizet, nec offerat, nec consecret, nec aedificet ecclesiam, donec permissionem acceperit ab episcopo illius provinciae, quia exemplum humilitatis est, nam qui sperat ab infidelibus aut laicis, et non ab episcopo permissionem accipit, infidelis (v 1, alienus) est.

plebem — We have translated this as 'community', and take the word in its political rather than its religious aspect. Cf Tirechan 20, *usque dum ad nostram plebem pervenerimus* where there can be no possibility of the religious meaning as the speaker has refused to become a Christian. We were tempted, therefore, to render *plebs* as *tuath*, but we found that Celtic scholars are by no means in agreement on the meaning of *tuath*.

baptizat — We can find no justification for the use of the indicative here. Bieler is probably right in regarding it as a case of regressive assimilation. Cf his introduction pp 38ff.

nec permissionem — We have followed Ware and the *Collectio Hibernensis* in translating as if we had *donec*. Spelman's *quam*, and Bieler's *quam ut* will also give the idea of 'not before', 'until'.

gentibus — In Canon 13, this word must mean 'heathen'. If this canon has the same origin, we would expect the same meaning here. If it does mean 'heathen', then this canon will be of fairly early date, when it was still possible for an intrusive newcomer to try to use local magnates to flout the authority of the established bishop. If the word means laymen, as Bieler translates it, then this canon will be of later date, implying a state of society that is already Christian, ie, probably post-Patrician. The collector of *Collectio Hibernensis* seems, himself, to have been in doubt as to the meaning, since he gives both meanings, *infidelibus aut laicis.*

religiosis hominibus — This is probably not a technical term equivalent to *monachis* as in *A Book of David*, Bieler, *Penitentials,* p 70 but merely means devout persons, cf Patrick, *Confessio* 49, *mulieribus religiosis.*

ordinare — Bieler's punctuation puts this word with *mos antiquis*, 'as the ancients used to decree', but he seems to translate it again with *pertinebunt*, 'shall be the bishop's to dispose of'. Haddan and Stubbs take it only with *pertinebunt*. We follow Bieler's punctuation.

pontifex, episcopus — We considered, but rejected for lack of supporting evidence, the possibility that these might be two persons, the *episcopus* the domestic bishop of a monastery, the *pontifex* the territorial bishop.

Assuming that these words refer to one person we found three possibilities:

(a) The bishop is *pontifex* in his sacral aspect, cf *Hebrews* 5, 1, and *episcopus* as administrator.

(b) Our author had the words *pontificalia dona* in mind and is in effect saying, 'these *pontificalia dona* belong to the bishop because he is the *pontifex*'. Against this is the fact that other similar canons which are more explicit on this matter do not use the term *pontificalia dona*, but, quoting passages of Scripture such as *Numbers* 18, 8, they use the words *decumae* and *primitiae*, cf *Apostolic Constitutions* 2, 24f.

(c) The canon derives from a continental source where the word *pontifex* was in use, and our compiler began with the unfamiliar word but then substituted the more familiar *episcopus* (Irish *epscop*). This gains support from the various *Concilia Aurelianensia. Aurelianense* IV has in separate canons *episcopus, pontifex, antistes* and *metropolitanus. Aurelianense* V, Canon 5, has both *episcopus* and *pontifex* in the same canon: *Ut nullus clericum seu lectorem alienum sine sui cessione pontificis vel promovere vel. . . . audeat vindicare . . . . Episcopus vero qui ordinaverit sex mensibus missas tantum facere non praesumat.* So also *Aurelianense* V, Canon 8: *Ut in civitate ubi pontifex iure humanae conditionis obierit nullus episcopus . . . ordinare clericos audeat.* In both these cases the *episcopus* and the *pontifex* are different individuals but not apparently different in rank. *Aurelianense* V is subscribed by fifty-one *episcopi* with no suggestion of primacy among them except that one manuscript has the list headed by Sacerdos of Lyons followed by Aurelian of Arles while another reverses these two. In various places the *Aurelianensia* have *sicut antiqui canones decreverunt* which may be the origin of *sicut mos antiquis* here.

CANON 26

This is set out in the manuscript as a separate canon, but appears to apply to the same situation as No. 25. That the Irish Church did bestow gifts on visiting dignitaries is clear from Adomnan, *Vita Columbae* 51A and 52A, where he shows us Columba (famous since Bede, *Historia Ecclesiastica* 3, 4 as not having been a bishop) receiving gifts — *xenia* — at Coleraine, about the year 575, in the presence of Bishop Conall, and again accepting gifts *ad cellam magnam Deathrib*, (which seems to have been Kilmore, situated below Lough Key near the Shannon). In both cases the gifts were specially collected for Columba. His gifts are called *xenia*. Perhaps if he had been a bishop, they might have been called *pontificalia*.

ab ecclesia sequestretur — We assume that this also means excommunication.

CANON 27

This is one of six canons (3, 24, 27, 30, 33, 34) which prohibit the activities of newcomers. Four of these canons (24, 30, 33, 34) imply that the prohibition might be waived if certain conditions were fulfilled, but Canon 27 appears, unconditionally, to prohibit the newcomer from the performance of any functions, presumably religious functions. It is conceivable that the prohibition applied only at the outset (perhaps the apparently superfluous *novus* is intended to make this clear) before the usual formalities of recognition had been completed.

It is thought that this canon may be a rider to Canon 24 which might refer to a community as a civil rather than ecclesiastical concept, whereas this would refer to a community with an established episcopal organisation. This interpretation requires that *aepiscopi* be taken to qualify *in plebe*, namely 'a bishop's diocese'. It may be, of course, that *aepiscopi* should be taken with *clericus*, the phrase meaning something like 'a bishop's chaplain', but it is difficult to envisage the circumstances in which a bishop's chaplain would be a *novus ingresor*, unless he were the chaplain of the visiting bishop referred to in Canon 30. To take *aepiscopi* with *in plebe* may be straining the order of the words, but the order of the whole phrase *Clericus . . . ingresor* is rather odd.

Other points which may be noted are:

(a) *clericus* is *nominativus pendens*, like *clericus* in Canon 33 and *diaconus* in Canon 34;

(b) *quislibet* is rare in this set of canons (see also Canons 29 and 30);

(c) *ingresor* is rare, if not a solecism;

(d) *aliquid* is used for *aliud* or *quicquam*.

CANON 28

Cf *Collectio Hibernensis XL, 9:*

(De eo, quod non debet excommunicatus offerre vel baptizare, sed solum orare) Patricius: Si quis excommunicatus fuerit, solus ex eadem hora orationem faciat, nec offerre nec baptizare liceat ei, donec se faciat emendatum.

This canon raises, in acute form, the question how far the text of *Collectio Hibernensis* may be used to 'correct' the reading of the manuscript. Syntactically, there is no need for the insertion of *fuerit*. The text of the manuscript gives a protasis running from *si* to *facit* and an apodosis from *nec offere* (*sic*) to *emendatum*. *facit* is more acceptable as the verb of a protasis than as a present of 'the done thing', for which there is no certain parallel in these canons (cf however Canon 24, *baptizat*). Since it has not been demonstrated that *Collectio Hibernensis* represents in general a more authentic tradition than our manuscript, and in this canon *solus ex eadem hora* inspires much less confidence than *solus in eadem domo cum fratribus*, it seems best to accept neither *fuerit* nor *ei* from *Collectio Hibernensis*.

The situation would seem to be one where a cleric is excluded from participation in the communal life of his brethren and, being penitent, is praying apart from them. In his unsupervised solitude he may be tempted to resume some of his former functions. This he must not do until he has performed his penance.

domo — The reference to a house may go back through the *Apostolic Canons* to *2 Epistle John* 10.

nec offere nec consecrare − The functions are, perhaps, those which a cleric on his own might readily perform. It is worth considering whether *consecrare* as well as *offere* refers to the Mass. Contrast the functions in Canons 24 and 27 and in *Collectio Hibernensis* (above).

qui si sic non fecerit − Although it is possible to defend the logic of this clause by referring it to *donec ... emendatum*, it seems better to compare Canon 27, *baptizare ... illum non licet ... qui si sic non faciat ...*

CANON 29

fratrum − From the context this must mean someone not yet baptized, but in normal patristic usage it always seems to mean exactly the opposite. Cf Augustine on *Psalm* 32,2,29: *neque enim dicimus eos (paganos) fratres nostros.* There is no indication of any special class of those who were disposed to be baptized. But presumably this is the sort of person meant. It seems to point to an early 'missionary' situation in the Irish Church rather than a later 'monastic' one.

.xl.mum − (a) The form: none of the dictionaries (Blaise, Niermeyer, Latham, Soutar) gives the form in − '*um*'. Presumably, in this case *ieiunium* would be understood, so that, although it is unusual, it is not grammatically impossible.

(b) Does this refer to Lent as we understand it; to one of the other forty-day fasts of the Celtic ecclesiastical year; or to a 'private' fast undertaken for the purpose of completing some particular penance?

(c) Bieler's most recent suggestion that *.xl.mum agat* means 'until he is 40 (?39) years old', cf 'St Patrick and the coming of Christianity' pp 88-9, does not commend itself to us any more than it did to Villanueva.

CANON 30

The canon appears to be related to 24 and 27, which also place restrictions on a visiting cleric. This canon refers only to two functions in the exercise of which the bishop is to be restricted − *ordinare* and *offerre*, and it is not clear why no reference is made to other episcopal functions.

nec − Either (a) = 'not' or (b) = 'not even' or (c) = 'neither'. If (a) or (b) is accepted the question remains why *ordinare* is singled out; if (c), what has become of the balancing *nec*(s)?

acciperit – The vowel after '*cc*' is either '*e*' written over an elongated '*i*' (or '*i*'), or vice versa. An apparent 'tail' to the '*a*' may be a cedilla and the possible '*i*' could, perhaps, be the '*i*' of an uncompleted *aecl* . . .

principatum – Editors since Spelman have omitted '*m*', which may be due to a mere scribal error or, on the other hand, to the late Latin tendency to confuse ablative and accusative.

susceptione – Presumably this noun corresponds to the verb *suscipere*, which is used of the reception of a stranger into a Christian community. In this case, the receiving bishop, as part of the act of *susceptio*, would invite the stranger to perform the functions proper to his status, cf Adomnan, *Vita Columbae* 45B.

hic – Either nominative, referring to the stranger, or adverbial, meaning 'in this parish (diocese)'.

CANON 31

It is hard to determine the relationship of this text to *Collectio Hibernensis* X, 10:

> *Clerici quos convenerit per discordiam aliquam, vel adprobatum fuerit uni vel duobus provocasse hostem ad interficiendum vel iniuriam faciendam homicidas magis congruum est nuncupari quam clericis et ab omnibus rectis habeantur alieni.*

The fact that the *Collectio Hibernensis* version is in the plural is interesting, because this is the second last of a long list of miscellaneous provisions on the behaviour of clerics, most of which are in the singular, so that if the compiler of *Collectio Hibernensis* was merely editing our version with a view to making it more grammatical, it seems odd that he should have turned it into the plural. It is tempting, with Bieler, to suppose that the *prolatum* of our manuscript represents the *probatum* of *Collectio Hibernensis* and that the *Collectio Hibernensis* is nearer to the archetype. Some slight support for this view may be found in the division and correction of *interficiendum*.

prolatum – Bieler suggests 'who has offered', a quasi-reflexive form. We take it with *per discordiam aliquam* 'impelled or induced by some quarrel'.

homicida – *congruum est* is being used after the fashion of *debet*. Even

Collectio Hibernensis, which uses the accusative *homicidas*, starts off with a nominative *Clerici*.

ab omnibus rectis habetur alienus — Bieler takes *ab omnibus rectis* as agent of *habetur*. It is just possible that it should be taken with *alienus*, cf Patrick, *Epistle*, ch 3, *a me alieni sunt et a Christo Deo meo*.

CANON 32

clericorum — As in Canons 25 and 28, one wonders how much weight should be given to the genitive. Taken strictly, it could mean any of the clerics, that is those of a given, and perhaps monastic, community. Otherwise it will mean merely 'any cleric'.

iuvare captivo — The dative appears to be used by analogy with the dative after *subvenire*.

suo praetio — Again, we must reject Bieler's translation 'money'. In the story of Libran in Adomnan, *Vita Columbae* 87A-91, Columba ransoms Libran by sending him back to his master in Ireland with the gift of a sword inlaid with ivory. The 'price of a man' was clearly a concept understood in Irish society, cf Patrick, *Confessio* 53: *pretium quindecim hominum*, and Muirchu, *Vita Patricii* 1, 10; *et portaret ei pretium suum*. In the *Penitentials*, in the estimates of commutation of penance, it still seems to be reckoned in terms of female slaves, *ancillae*. It is not clear whether *suo* refers to the cleric or to the captive. If to the cleric, it would mean 'honour price'. Perhaps the sword mentioned above would have been more appropriate to the rank of the priest Columba of the Ui Neill than to Libran, who worked for many years in a reed-plot, but we do not know enough about the economics of the period to be sure. On the whole, we thought it more likely that *suo* referred, albeit ungrammatically, to the captive.

inviolaverit — Bieler follows Salmasius as recorded by Wilkins in reading *involaverit*, and translating 'kidnaps'. We thought that the reading might have been *violaverit* 'uses violence', the *'in'* being a scribe's error, a form of dittography of the following *'vi'*.

CANON 33

This is one of six canons (3, 24, 27, 30, 33 and 34) which define the rights of a cleric who comes from outside, but this is the only one which specifies the origin of the newcomers. We had independently reached the same view as Kenney (*Sources*, p 170) that *Britanis* is from *Britannia*, not from *Britannus*, the plural representing the five provinces of Britain mentioned in the *Notitia Dignitatum*. Otherwise, it is hard to see why our document uses the 'classical' form *Britannus*, instead of the much commoner colloquial form *Brito*, for an inhabitant of the larger island. We also agree with Kenney that this cleric is more likely to have been a refugee from the English invasions, rather than someone suspect, as not conforming to orthodox usage, after the Irish Church in the mid-seventh century had accepted the Roman Easter and tonsure – a view put forward by Haddan and Stubbs.

clericus – As in Canon 27, we have *clericus* as a hanging nominative followed by *non licitum (*sc. *est) = non debet.*

ministrare – We take this to mean to minister, ie, to perform clerical functions. We assume that a properly accredited cleric (*cum epistola*) would be permitted to minister, but that the unaccredited are merely to be given asylum in the community.

CANON 34

Cf Collectio Hibernensis XXXIX, 11:

Monachus inconsulto abbate vagus ambulans in plebe debet excommunicari.

nobiscum similiter – This suggests that this canon should be taken closely with the previous one, or at least with some canon which dealt with the position of external clergy.

parruchiam – In Canon 30 we took this to be 'diocese', but it is possible that here it should be taken to refer to the monastic usage of *parruchia* to describe the group or family of monasteries having a common foundation, cf Tirechan, *Vita Patricii*, ch 18. Then it would not be necessary to excise the words *inconsultu suo abbate*, as Bieler, *Penitentials*, p 240 suggests. A deacon would be allowed to travel from one monastery to another within the *parruchia* only with his abbot's written permission.

adsentiat – The best we can do with this verb is to assume that it is a single instance of a verb meaning to adhere to or join, just as Blaise records a single instance of *absentiare*

nec cibum ministrare – We cannot accept Bieler's translation (*Penitentials*): 'he is not even to be given food' as being too much at variance with the native convention of the duty of hospitality. We take the verb to be used actively, meaning 'to serve food', a typical example of the deacon's duties. Cf *Collectio Hibernensis* III, 2, *ministrare mensis*, which quotes *Acts* 6, 2 with reference to this function. We also take *nec* to mean merely 'not', balancing the following *et*.

BIBLIOGRAPHY

Modern works cited are listed here. Elsewhere abbreviated references are given. Ancient works are included, in alphabetical order of authors' names, only where citation is from a specific modern edition.

Adomnan, Life of Columba, Ed. Anderson, London 1961.

Baxter J.H., Johnson C. and others, Medieval Latin Word-list from British and Irish Sources, Oxford 1932.

Best R.I., 'The Settling of the Manor of Tara', Ériu 4, 1912.

Bieler L., The Life and Legend of St. Patrick, Dublin 1949.
'Fernassimilation und Reimzwang', Classica et Mediaevalia 15, 1954.
The Irish Penitentials, The Institute for Advanced Studies, Dublin 1949.
'Patrick's Synod, a Revision', Mélanges offertes à Mlle. Christine Mohrmann, Utrecht 1963.
The Works of St. Patrick, Westminster, Maryland 1963.
'Interpretationes Patricianae', Irish Ecclesiastical Record 107, Jan.–June 1967.
'St. Patrick and the Coming of Christianity' (A History of Irish Catholicism Vol. I,1) Dublin 1967.

Binchy D.A., 'Patrick and his Biographers', Studia Hibernica 2, 1962.
'St. Patrick's "First Synod" ', Studia Hibernica 8, 1968.

Blaise A., Dictionnaire latin-francais des Auteurs Chrétiens, Strasbourg 1954.

Bradshaw H., The Early Collection of Canons known as Hibernensis, Cambridge 1893.

Bury J.B., The Life of St. Patrick and his Place in History, London 1905.

Charlemagne, Capitulare Saxonicum, Monumenta Germaniae Historica, Hanover 1881.

Conchubranus, Vita Monennae, Ed. Esposito, Proc. R.I.A. XXVIII(C), 1910.

Ernout A. and Thomas F., Syntaxe latine, 2nd Ed. Paris 1964.

Festus, De Verborum Significatu, Ed. Lindsay, Leipsic 1913.

Gaudemet J., L'Eglise dans L'Empire Romain, Paris 1955.

Gervase of Tilbury, Ed. Stevenson, London 1875.

Gregory of Tours, Ed. Levison, Monumenta Germaniae Historica, Hanover 1965.

Haddan A.W. and Stubbs W., Councils and Ecclesiastical Documents relating to Great Britain and Ireland, Oxford 1878.

Hughes K., The Church in Early Irish Society, London 1966.

James M.R., A Descriptive Catalogue of Mss. in the Library of Corpus Christi College Cambridge, Vol II, 1912.

Kenney J.F., The Sources for the Early History of Ireland (Ecclesiastical), Dublin 1966.

Lindsay W., Syntax of Plautus, Oxford 1907.

Lombard Laws, Ed. Muratori, Rerum Italicarum Scriptores, Bologna 1900.

Löfstedt E., Philologischer Kommentar zur Peregrinatio Aetheriae, Oxford 1936.

Meyer K. and others, Contributions to a Dictionary of the Irish Language, R.I.A., Dublin 1912 onwards.

McKenna L. Iomarbhágh na bhFileadh, The Contentio of the Bards, Irish Text Society Vol. XX, London 1918.

Meyer-Lubke W., Romanisches Etymologisches Wörterbuch, Heidelberg 1911.

Mohrmann C., Etudes sur le Latin des Chrétiens, Rome 1958-65.
    The Latin of St. Patrick, Dublin 1961.

Nerney D.S., A Study of St. Patrick's Sources, Irish Ecclesiastical Record 71 and 72, Jan.-June and July-Dec. 1949.

Plummer C., Vitae Sanctorum Hiberniae, Oxford 1910.

Powicke F.M. and Cheney C.R., Councils and Synods with Documents relating to the English Church, 2nd Ed. Oxford 1954.

Prou M., Les Monnaies Carolingiennes, Paris 1969.

Spelman H., Collection of Decrees Laws etc. relating to the British Church, London 1639.

Strachan J., Old Irish Glosses, Dublin 1904.

Summers A.M., The Vampire, his Kith and Kin, London 1928.

Thurneysen R., Old Irish Reader, Dublin 1949.

Villanueva J.L., Sancti Patricii Synodi Canones Opuscula, Dublin 1835.

Waddel H., The Wandering Scholars, London 1927.

Ware J., S. Patricio adscripta Opuscula, London 1656.

Wasserschleben F.W.H., Die Bussordnungen der abendländischen Kirche, Halle 1851.

Die Irische Kannonensammlung (Collectio Canonum Hibernensis), 2nd Ed. Leipsic 1885.

Wilkins D., Concilia Magnae Britanniae et Hiberniae, London 1737.

Woodcock E.C., A New Latin Syntax, London 1959.

GRATIAS

AGIMUS DO PATRI
ET FILIO ET SPU SCO
PRESBITERIS ET DIACONIB:
ET OMNI CLERO PATRICIUS
AUXILIUS ISSERNINUS
EPISCOPI SALUTEM

Satius nobis neglezentes
promonere culpas qui facta sunt
Solamone dicente melius est
arguere quam irasci exem
pla difinitionis nostrae in
ferius conscripta sunt. et sic
inchoant.

Siquis in questionem captiuis
quesierit in plebe suo iure sine
permisione itruis excommunicari
Lectores denique cognoscant
unusquisque ecclm in qua psallat

INCIPIT.

SINODVS

IRSCO

PORV̄

IDEST

PATRICII AVXILII ISSERNINI

C lericus uagus non sit in plebe

S iquis permissione acciperit & col
lectum sit pretium non plus exigat
quam qd necessitas poscit

S iquid supra manserit ponat sup
altare pontificis uidetur aliundi
genti
Q uicumq; clericus ab hostiario
usque ad sacerdotem sine tunica
uisus fuerit atq; turpitudine ue
tris & nuditate non tegat. Et si non
more romano capilli eius tonsisin
E t uxor eius si nuelato capite ambu
lauerit pariter a laicis contempno
tur & ab ecclesia separentur

Q uicuq; clericus ussus neglegen
tie causa ad collectas mane uel
uespere non occurrerit alienus
habeatur nisi forte iugo serui tu
tis sit detentur

C lericus si progenitali homine P

fideiusor fuerit inquacuique
quantitate. &sicontigerit qd
mirum nonpotest perastutiam
aliquam gentilis ille clerico fallat
rebuffatis. clericus ille soluat debi
tum. Nam si armis conpugnaue
rit cum illo merito extraecclesiam
conputetur.

Monachus & uirgo unus abhinc
& alia abaliunde inuno hospi
tia nonconmaneant nec inuno
curru. Auilla inuilla discurrent
nec adsidue inuicem confabula
tionem exerceant

Si incoeptum boni operis rosten
derit inpsallendo. et nunc inter
misit & comam habeat abecclesia
excludendus nisi fatuti priori
se restituerit

Quicumque clericus abaliquo

excōmonicatus fuerit &aluseū
susciperit ambo coēqualipeniten
tia   utantur .

Quicumq; xp̄ianus excominica
tus fuerit necetur elimosina
recipiatur

Elimosinam agentibus offerendā
in ecclesiam recipi non licet

Xp̄ianus qui occiderit aut fornica
tione fecerit aut more gentalium
ad aruspicem iurauerit per sin
gula cremina annūpenitentiae
agat: impleto cum testibus uenit
anno penitentiae &postea resol
uetur asacerdote

Et qui furtum fecerit demedium
penitteat .xx. diebus cū pane &si
fieri potest rapta repsentet
si in ecclesiam renuetur

Xp̄ianus qui crediderit ēelami ā

insaeculo quaecumterptatur striga

Anathematandus: quicumque sup

Animã famamistam inposuerit,

necante inecclesiã recipiendusque

utidem creminisquodfecit suaiterũ

uoce reuocet & sicpoenitentiã cum

omni diligentia agat

Uirgo quæuouerit dõ permanet kasta.

Et postea nubserit carnalẽ sponsũs

excommonis sit donecconuertatur

siconuersa fuerit. etdimiserit ad

ulterium penitentiã agat. etpostea

non inuna doma necinuna uilla

habitent:

Siquisexcõmonis fuerit necnocte

pascharum inecclm nonintroeat

donec penitentiã recipiat

Mulier xpiana quae acceperituirũ

honestis nuptis & postmodũ discer

serit aprimo &iunxerit seadultẽ

rio que haec fecit excomonis sit

X pianus qui fraudat debitum cuius
liber rtu genoliu . excomonis sit
donec soluat debitum

X pianus cui dereliquerit aliquis et
prouocat eum inductum & ñ in
ecctm utibi examinetur . causa
quisic fecerit alienus sit

S iquis tradiderit filiasua uiro hones
tis nuptis & amauerit aliu & con
sentit filiae suae . et acceperit doñ
ambo abiecta excludantur

S iquis prbiteroru ecclesiā edifica
uerit ñ offerat antequa adducat
suum pontifice uteam consecret
quia sic decet

S iquis aduena ingressus fuerit ple
bem nonante baptizat nequeoffe
rat nec consecret nec ecclesiā
aedificet nec pmissione accipiat

ab episcopo non namquia gentibus
sperat permissionē alienus sit
Sique a religiosis hominibus do
nata fuerint diebusillis quibus
pontifex insigulis habitauerit
aecclesis pontificalia dona sicut
mos antiquis ordinare ad episcopum per tinebunt siueadus
sum necessariū siue egentibus
distribuendū · prouti ipse eps
moderabit
Siquis uero clericus contraue
nerit · etdona inuadere fuerit
dephensus atturpis lucri cupi
dus abecclesia sequestretur ·
Clericus episcopū inplebe quis
libet nouus ingressor baptizari
et offerre illum nonliceat nec
aliquid agere quisi sic non faciat
excommonis sit

Siquis clericorū excōmmonis
solus non in eadem domo acū fra
tribus oratione facit nec offere
nec consecrare licet donec se faciat
emendatum · qui sisic sū fecerit
dupliciter uindicetur

Siquis fratrum accipere gratiā di
uoluerit non ante baptizetur
quam ut xlmum agat

Aepiscopus quis libet quidesua
in alterā progreditur parruchiā
nec ordinare psumat nisi pmissio
nem acceperit abeo qui insuo
principatum ē · die dominica
offerat tantum susceptione
& obsequi hic contentus sit

Siquis conduxerit eduobus cle
ricis quos discordare conuenit
per discordia aliquā prolatū
uni eduobus hostem ad intersi

ciendum homicida congruū ē
nominari quiclericus ab omnib;
rectis habetur. Alienus
Siquis clericorū uoluerit iuuare
captiuo cum suo ptio illi subue
niat. Nam sip fur tū illū inuio
lauerit blasfemantur multi
clerici per unum latronem qui
sic fecerit excommonissit
Clericus qui debritanis ad nos uenerit
sine epistola. & si habitat in plebe
non licitum ministrare
Diaconus nobiscū similiter qui in
consultu suo abbate sine litteris
in aliam parruchiam ad sentiat.
nec cibum ministrare decet. Et
a suo pbitero quem contempsit
perpenitentiam uindicetur.
Et monachus inconsultu abbate
uagulus decet uindicari

FINIT SINODI DIS TITUTA.

INCIPIUNT AGUSTINI DICTA.
DECOG.UM RATIONE

Qualis

Qalis esse debet quae uxor
habenda est secundu legem.
uirgo casta etsponsata in
uirginitate. etdotata legitime.
etaparentibus tradita adspon
so. etparanimpis accipienda.
etita secundu legem eteuan
gelium publicis nuptis honesta
inconiugio licite sumenda.
Et omnibus dieb; uitae nisi excon
sensu &causa uacandidō num
quam propter hominem sepa
randa. Etsifornicata fuerit
dimittenda. sedilla uiuente
altera nonducenda: quiaad
ulteri regnum dī nonposside
bunt. etpenitentia illius